Rio
de Janeiro

Front cover: View of Corcovado
with Sugar Loaf beyond

Right: The Cristo Redentor statue

TOP 10 ATTRACTIONS

Zona Sul • From Copacabana to Ipanema, its beaches are fabled the world over *(page 32)*

New Year celebrations • Known as Reveillon, they are among the most spectacular in the world *(page 79)*

Cristo Redentor • Located atop Corcovado, this icon of the city was named one of the New Seven Wonders of the World in 2007 *(page 29)*

Petrópolis • This lovely old city was once the summer residence of emperors and presidents *(page 65)*

Sugar Loaf Take a cable car to the top to see panoramic Rio at its finest *(page 28)*

Centro Histórico Reminders of old Rio abound *(page 42)*

Botanical Garden Hundreds of colourful tropical plants and birds in the middle of the city *(page 37)*

Costa Verde The paradisiacal coastline beyond Rio *(page 60)*

Nightlife The hedonistic spirit of Carnaval spills over into Rio's pulsating bar, music and dance scene *(page 81)*

Carnaval Outrageous costumes, non-stop music, wild dancing: five days and nights of raucous revelry *(page 73)*

CONTENTS

13

86

97

9

68

48

INTRODUCTION

Rio de Janeiro's natural beauty is so exalted that the presence of a towering statue of Christ the Redeemer, high on Corcovado mountain overlooking the city, doesn't seem the least bit surprising. Arms outstretched, *Cristo Redentor* (Christ the Redeemer), one of the New Seven Wonders of the World, blesses the city on a daily basis. But abundantly blessed it already is. This city of 10 million is sprinkled delicately among curves of gorgeous bays, sweeping white-sand beaches, coastal mountains swathed in tropical rainforest, and islands that ripple out to the sea.

Residents call their city simply *Rio* ('hee-ooh'). But *cariocas*, as the locals are called, sometimes can't resist a dose of grandiosity when they speak of the special place they call home. To them, Rio is *cidade maravilhosa* – the marvellous city.

Exotic flora at the Botanical Garden

Rio's magnetism has drawn settlers and visitors for centuries. The city is without a doubt one of the world's most photographed, and photogenic, places. Who hasn't seen a picture of Sugar Loaf, Guanabara Bay and the magnificent urban beaches? Or heard about the teensy bikinis, the firm bodies, and Carnaval, where a party-till-your-sequins-drop-off attitude reigns? All over the world, the words Copacabana and Ipanema roll off the tongue like universal shorthand for exotica.

Colonial houses on Largo do Boticário

Rio is lined with some 90km (56 miles) of beaches; nearly one-fifth of the city is tropical forest. Thanks to the climate and the body-beautiful fixation of *cariocas*, the city is passionate about outdoor sports. Early in the morning and well into the night, joggers compete with cyclists and in-line skaters along the beachfronts. Year-round, surfers and windsurfers navigate the waves, while hang-glider pilots execute lazy turns high above the sands.

In addition to its beaches and panoramic vistas, Rio also has numerous historic churches, excellent examples of colonial and fin-de-siècle architecture, fine museums, diverse restaurants, addictive dance halls and, of course, the sultry

Beach Culture

To really understand Rio and the *cariocas*, you'll have to hang out at the beach. *Cariocas* adore the sun and the deep colour it gives to the already stunning spectrum of skin tones on display. Brilliant sun, usually not much of a rarity in Rio, causes most *cariocas* to drop what they're doing and make a beeline to the beach. This is one city where the natives are just as keen on beach life as the tourists.

Rio's beaches are a microcosm of life here. The beach is the engine behind social encounters. So if you go to the beach expecting to kick back with an umbrella and a book, you'll be distracted. Rio's beaches are a parade of bodies in constant motion. Catch the dog walkers, on the left. Surfers carrying their boards, straight ahead. Bronzed *cariocas* in the tiniest of *tanguinhas* (bikinis) slathering on the suntan lotion. Volleyball games in all directions. Barefoot vendors of *guaraná* (a caffeine-laced soft drink), *cerveja* (beer), and *cangas* (colourful cover-ups) at 6 o'clock. Even businessmen toting briefcases and negotiating deals will be somewhere. Overhead, aeroplanes carry banners touting films or beer or a new shopping mall. Muscle-men bob up and down on the chin-up bars near the pavement, and behind them, roller-bladers and joggers and cyclists cruise by.

rhythms of samba, *pagode* and bossa nova.

Cariocas inject the city with its special rhythm, its vibrance, its sport and its song. Life here is not to be observed, it is to be consumed, and the bolder the appetite, the better. Don't be surprised if you hear a beach vendor imploring people to '*Tirar roupa! Tirar roupa!*' (Take off your clothes!). This is a decidedly tropical and sensual place, where too many clothes are not just impractical, but a hindrance.

While they are every bit as romantic as Parisians, as animated as Romans and as nocturnal as Madrid's night

Beach life

owls, *cariocas* are unique. Exuberant almost to the point of caricature, they embrace the present like no one else. *Now* is the time to share a beer with a friend, dance a nostalgic *sambinha* (little samba), and slip out of work early and head to the beach. Such spontaneity is startling but addictive for visitors from more systematic and sober societies.

Location and Climate

Rio lies on the Atlantic Ocean, somewhat more than halfway down Brazil's eastern coast and very nearly smack on the Tropic of Capricorn. The coastal mountain ranges consist of granite peaks draped in lush tropical rainforest. The peaks, which include the famous Sugar Loaf (Pão de Açúcar), Cor-

Carnaval revellers sporting Flamengo football club colours

covado, Dois Irmãos and flat-topped Gávea, dramatically hug the sea and give Rio its signature beauty.

Rio is about as close to the equator as Havana, so winter is a mere formality. In July (the worst of winter south of the equator), the average temperature dips to only 20°C (69°F). This scarcely interferes with the outdoor way of life; the beaches are crowded most of the year. While summer, which runs from late December to late March, brings the *cariocas* to the beaches in unrelenting waves, it can be frighteningly hot and humid for wintering travellers from northern Europe and North America.

When the weather begins to heat up around October, it's a sign for *cariocas* that Carnaval is on its way. Beginning in November, behind-the-scenes activities of Carnaval begin. As the weeks go by, excitement spreads to every neighbourhood. The powder keg of passion finally ignites during the last five days before Lent, when everybody joins the round-the-clock spree. With its frenzy of *bateria* (percussion), limber-legged dancing, singing, and resplendent costumes and bodies, Rio's annual extravaganza is one of life's overwhelming experiences.

Population and Religion

Carnaval's inclusive nature is one of the best expressions of Brazil's diversity. Like the rest of Brazil, Rio is a cultural stew of colours and races: indigenous, black, European and everything between.

The original inhabitants of Brazil were Indians. In the 16th century, the Portuguese colonised the country, enslaved the Indians, and established the Catholic religion and Portuguese language and culture in what would become South America's biggest nation. The indigenous population, estimated at up to five million, was drastically reduced. Today only about 410,000 remain, yet their lands cover 12 percent of Brazilian territory, or an area larger than France and the UK combined.

When the sugar mills and coffee plantations needed more manpower than the indigenous Indians could supply, black slaves were brought from Africa. Most modern immigration to Brazil occurred between 1850 and 1950; during that period, nearly five million immigrants came from Europe, mostly from Italy, Portugal and Spain.

Today, about a third of Brazilians are *mestiços*, of mixed Portuguese and Indian origin. Slightly more than half are white or predominantly white. Afro-Brazilians make up slightly more than 10 percent of the population.

Good luck gift

Even the most sophisticated *carioca* probably has a *figa*, an amulet in the form of a fist with the thumb extended between the second and third fingers. This Afro-Brazilian symbol, a remnant of the slave trade, serves to ward off the evil eye and ensure luck and fertility. For it to work, however, it must be received as a gift.

Music, religion, sport and language have all benefited from the intermingling of peoples in Brazil, and Brazilians have, at least on the surface, achieved a remarkable level of racial harmony. Despite the assertion of some Brazilians that their society is raceless, however, Afro-Brazilians suffer from an acute form of economic racism. What is more, in the past, Brazil's track record of dealing with indigenous peoples has not been a very distinguished one.

Religion reflects the nation's mixture of races and cultures. Most Brazilians are still Roman Catholic, a religion imposed by the Portuguese and later reaffirmed by waves of European immigrants. But Catholicism, once the religion of 95 percent of Brazilians, has, since the 1970s, seen many of its adherents transfer their allegiance to various Protestant denominations. Pentecostal groups in particular have grown dramatically, especially among the poor. In every town, you'll find makeshift churches with names like Assembléia de Deus.

Afro-Brazilian culture and religion infuse the whole of Brazilian society. African slaves brought to Brazil succeeded in merging their own native beliefs with Western beliefs and practices in a particularly vibrant example of religious syncretism. It's common for descendants of these slaves to appeal to both Western saints and *orixás* (spirits and divinities) in their devotions. From religion to language to music, African beliefs and traditions have informed much of modern Brazilian culture.

Football

As the land of *Rei* (king) Pelé and as five-time winners of the World Cup, which it will host in 2014, Brazil is also famous for its football. If you attend a match at Maracanã Stadium, you'll see some of the soccer wizardry that stops opposing teams and, at World Cup time, the whole of Brazil, dead in its tracks. At even the most routine match, you'll encounter fans who are downright obsessive about the game.

Guanabara Bay with Botafogo Beach and Sugar Loaf

But you don't need to go to Maracanã to find good football playing. Young footballers do their best impersonations of Pelé, Ronaldo and the other Brazilian greats on the beach even on days so torrid it's an effort just to flag down the soft-drink pedlar. And on warm nights, beneath the floodlamps on Copacabana and Ipanema beaches, teams go at it until midnight.

Beyond Rio

Finally, for those with more than a few days to spend in the city, Rio lies in a privileged position for day trips and overnight side trips. To the east and west along the coasts of the state of Rio de Janeiro, the beaches just keep getting better. West of Rio is the stunning Costa Verde (Green Coast), with a series of paradisiacal stretches where lush vegetation and mountains meet perfect sands and transparent waters – forming a green, white and blue striped flag that might as well be the official colours of the state of Rio de Janeiro. The standouts include Ilha Grande, plunked down in a bay that features a supporting cast of 360 other islands, and the perfectly-preserved colonial town of Paraty. Northeast of Rio is the chic coastal resort of Búzios, a beautiful playground for beautiful people.

Rio is much more than the sum of its coasts, though. Just an hour from Rio is the relaxed European mountain retreat of Petrópolis, where Emperor Dom Pedro II had his summer palace. The Paraíba Valley is where Brazil's coffee barons reigned in the 19th century until their source of cheap labour, the large, strong slave population, was set free. Today you can visit a number of impressive coffee plantations, or *fazendas*, some of which have been opened to visitors for overnight stays.

No matter where you go and what you do, though, you'll remember the people of Rio. Smiles come easily in spite of the state of the economy, crime figures, the housing crisis and, for most, woeful educational and job opportunities. Some Brazilians deride themselves for being overly passive, allowing inequality to persist and politicians to get away with frankly undemocratic behaviour. Yet it is also true that *cariocas* have a remarkable ability to live determinedly in the moment, look beyond their city's shortcomings, and celebrate the joy of living in one of the world's most spectacular locations.

Read the signs

Cariocas are big on body language and hand signals. After just a couple of days, you'll find yourself giving the thumbs-up signal, just as they do, to communicate 'OK' or 'thank you'. However, if you touch your forefinger to your thumb – the American equivalent of 'A-OK' – you'll basically be telling people where they can stick it.

A BRIEF HISTORY

The Portuguese explorer Pedro Álvares Cabral discovered Brazil in 1500, which was convenient for the generations of schoolchildren who had to memorise the date in history classes. That Cabral didn't actually set foot in Brazil until after the terms of the Treaty of Tordesillas were in force certainly benefited the Portuguese empire. Under this 1494 pact, Portugal and Spain had grandly divided the presumed spoils of the New World – by drawing a vertical line down a still-empty map. The Brazilian coast neatly dropped into the eastern zone, reserved, sight unseen, for Portugal.

Cabral was not initially impressed by his discovery when he landed just south of Porto Seguro in what is today the state of Bahia. He mistakenly thought he had found an island, not the South American mainland. And, having hoped to exploit the riches of the Orient, he was disappointed to meet with savages similar to the ones Columbus called Indians. Those in Vera Cruz (True Cross), as Brazil was first known, belonged mainly to the Tupi-Guarani family of tribes; they would later intermarry with the predominantly male settlers, producing the beginnings of the racially mixed society that has come to characterise Brazil.

The voyage of Cabral

Successive expeditions reported only one resource of commercial interest, the tree named *pau-brasil* (brazil-wood). The country was named for the tree, which produced red and purple

River of January

The naming of Rio de Janeiro was based on a misunderstanding. A popular version says Gonçalo Coelho, the Portuguese navigator who first reached Guanabara Bay, mistakenly thought it was the mouth of a great river. He looked at his calendar and proclaimed it the 'River of January' (*Rio de Janeiro* in Portuguese).

dyes, not the other way around. Brazil held rich agricultural promise, but its potential took time to discover due to a series of misguided attempts to speculate on single-crop agriculture: first sugar, then coffee and later rubber. Today Brazil is one of the world's great agricultural powerhouses.

Guanabara Bay, the location of Rio de Janeiro, was first reached by the Portuguese navigator Gonçalo Coelho on New Year's Day, 1502, but there was no attempt to establish any form of settlement. Indeed, half a century was to pass before a town came to be founded on the beautiful bay.

French Threats

To the dismay of Lisbon, the pioneer was a French admiral, Nicolas Durand de Villegaignon, and to the dismay of Rome, the French settlers included a colony of Protestants. The twin challenges of what was provocatively named *la France Atlantique* spurred Portugal to military action, which continued intermittently for several years. The French were finally dislodged on 20 January 1567. In the hour of victory, an arrow mortally wounded the leader of the Portuguese forces, Estácio de Sá. As this was the day of the Italian martyr, St Sebastian, he became Rio's patron saint. Consequently the official name of the city is still São Sebastião do Rio de Janeiro.

After the French fled, the Brazilian governor general, Mem de Sá, moved the city's administrative centre from the base of the spectacular Sugar Loaf mountain to a less vulnerable location on the hill known as Morro do Castelo. No sign of this hill exists today; it was bulldozed to provide landfill to extend the modern metropolis into the bay, but it would have sat in front of what is today Santos Dumont Airport. Mem de Sá, who just happened to be the uncle of the fallen Está-cio de Sá, appointed Salvador Corrêa de Sá to be captain of the colony. Salvador was also a nephew of Mem de Sá. Nepotism would be a familiar feature of Brazilian political and economic life for many years.

As news of the discovery of gold in nearby Minas Gerais fil-tered through to Europe, so the interest in Rio de Janeiro grew proportionately. The French put the city under siege unsuc-cessfully in 1710, but a year later the privateer René Duguay-Trouin was more successful. Although his sizable flotilla was sighted approaching Guanabara Bay, the governor, Castro Morais, failed to organise a coherent defence plan. Rio was

Church of St Anthony, built in the early 17th century

captured. According to the Brazilian chronicles, the French sacked the town and took what was left in ransom. Duguay-Trouin's fleet, now laden with booty, including 200 head of cattle, 100 crates of sugar and 1,000 *cruzados*, slipped away before Portuguese reinforcements could arrive. For bungling the defence, Castro Morais was banished from the city.

Capital City

The cultivation of sugar cane, and later sensational discoveries of gold and diamonds, made Brazil an economically interesting proposition in the 17th and 18th centuries. African slaves were imported to work the cane fields. They mixed with the white and Indian populations of the territory.

Brazil was elevated from the status of a colony to a vice-royalty, and in 1763 the capital was moved from Salvador (Bahia) to Rio de Janeiro, which was closer to the gold and

Royal barge on display in the Espaço Cultural da Marinha

diamonds. Rio remained a small and easy-going tropical town, lacking much in the way of amenities. The first viceroy to take up residence, a fastidious nobleman, hastily moved house from what he considered the loathsome, swampy Guanabara bayfront to the relatively fresh air of nearby hills. Rio's role as a great cosmopolitan capital could hardly have been imagined until the new century changed the map of Europe.

Napoleon was on the move, doing everything he could to seal the European continent off from England. Portugal refused to fall into line, so Marshal Andoche Junot and his formidable army crossed Spain and invaded, aiming for Lisbon. The Portuguese royal court made a quick decision to stage a strategic retreat to a safe haven across the sea. In 1807 Dom João of Portugal, who served as regent for his mother, the mentally ill Queen Maria I, chose Brazil. He and 15,000 members of the court and its support staff sailed from Lisbon on 29 November 1807. Stopping first in Salvador, where he signed a decree opening the Brazilian ports to his allies, Dom João disembarked in Rio on 8 March 1808 to become the only European monarch of the time to rule his empire from a colony.

Even after Portugal's liberation from Napoleon, Dom João decided to remain in Brazil, and when 'Mad Maria' died in 1818, he was crowned king in Rio's Igreja do Carmo (Carmelite Church). João VI was a popular monarch, and during his reign Rio began to take on the appearance of a civilised city, giving foundation to an academy of fine arts, a national museum, a botanical garden, a bank and a newspaper.

Brazilian Empire

In 1821 Dom João was induced to return to Lisbon and assume control of his country, so he handed over Brazil to his eldest son, Dom Pedro, and Pedro's bride, who was the Archduchess Leopoldina Josepha Carolina of Habsburg, the daughter of the Emperor of Austria. Though Leopoldina was definitely no beauty (Pedro had wed her by proxy on the basis of a flagrantly retouched portrait) she was a popular queen who produced the first Brazilian-born heir to the throne.

Relations between Portugal and Brazil deteriorated rapidly, and in 1822, with pressure building in Brazil for independence, King Pedro leapt aboard the bandwagon. Tearing Portuguese medals and emblems from his uniform, he proclaimed, 'Independence or death!' He was crowned emperor of Brazil. Three years later, thanks to heavy pressure from Austria and Britain, the Portuguese government officially acknowledged the independence of Brazil. When King João died in 1826, his son, Pedro I of Brazil, assumed the additional title of Pedro IV of Portugal, which he passed on to his daughter, Maria da Gloria, with his younger brother, Miguel, acting as regent.

But Pedro's Brazilian subjects began to grow restless at his stubborn, autocratic rule. Faced with a military coup in 1831, he abdicated on 7 April in favour of his five-year-old son, who became Pedro II. The dethroned father sailed to Portugal to fight for the crown of the mother country, which he won for his daughter after a long and bitter civil war.

The future Pedro II held by his mother, Maria Leopoldina

Golden Age

Pedro II was declared of age in 1840, some months prior to his 15th birthday, and ruled for nearly half a century more, during which Rio de Janeiro grew and prospered. Fish-oil lamps gave way to gaslight on the streets

Rio, seen from Santa Teresa, in 1883

of the capital, and by 1872 the population had climbed to 275,000. Steamboats linked Rio and Europe – not to mention Rio and Niterói across the bay – and horse-drawn trams brought mass transport to the metropolis. Matching this technological progress, the city's social growth was marked by the foundation of schools, colleges, institutes and hospitals.

Under Pedro's reign, traditional absolutism evolved into a parliamentary monarchy with a two-party system. In 1850 the slave trade was outlawed, but the emperor was determined to push his country towards the total abolition of slavery. The end of the struggle came in 1888. At the time, Pedro was abroad, so the abolition law was signed by his daughter, acting as regent; consequently she was dubbed Isabel the Redeemer.

Fierce opposition from slave-owners added to the smouldering dissatisfactions of feuding politicians and military men. The anti-monarchical pot finally boiled over in November 1889. With the emperor at the summer palace in

Petrópolis, plotters in Rio de Janeiro set in motion a blood-less coup. On 15 November, Pedro was forced to abdicate and the royal family was expelled from the country within 48 hours before counter-revolutionary forces could rally round the crown. The victors proclaimed a federal republic, to be called the United States of Brazil, while the emperor and his family went into exile in France.

20th-Century Rio

In the first decade of the 20th century, Rio de Janeiro began to take on the appearance of a modern capital city. A wide, straight main street, now called Avenida Rio Branco, was paved. Two tunnels brought Copacabana within easier reach of the business district. The port of Rio was developed; immigration ran at about 100,000 a year. A crash pro-gramme of sanitation eradicated outbreaks of yellow fever by 1907, when the capital's population stood at 800,000.

World War I proved a boon to the Brazilian economy. Exports to the Allies multiplied, and industry expanded to fill the gap in imports.

Flying Down to Rio

In the early 1920s, Avenida Atlântica, in Copacabana, was lined with the private houses of adventurous Cariocas. The first hotel, the grand, stark white Copacabana Palace, was inaugurated in 1923 and was the back drop to the first film to pair Fred Astaire and Ginger Rogers, *Flying Down To Rio*. The hotel quickly attracted the likes of Roosevelt and de Gaulle, Eva Perón and Lana Turner, Chiang Kai-shek and Emperor Hirohito. If they came to Rio, they stayed at the Cop Palace. The presence of these famous faces brought worldwide fame to Copacabana. Visiting kings, stars and multinational magnates still turn up at the Cop Palace, now part of the Orient-Express group, and it remains the most elegant hotel in town.

The New York stock-market crash of 1929 sent shock waves as far south as Rio. The bottom fell out of the coffee market, and the rest of Brazilian agriculture and industry suffered. It was a moment ripe for political turmoil. Plots and counterplots were being hatched, and finally a revolution overthrew the government. A junta of military officers based in Rio

The Copacabana Palace hotel

gave power to a tough politician from the Gaucho country of Rio Grande do Sul, Getúlio Vargas.

In 1937 Vargas inaugurated the Estado Nôvo (New State), involving a continuous state of emergency, censorship and, for serious offences like assassinating the president, the revival of the death penalty. A decree that photographs of the dictator had to be displayed in public places, including business premises, set the tone for his administration.

Under the Vargas regime, Brazil joined the Allies in World War II, becoming the only Latin American country to take an active part in the war. Brazilian troops arrived in Italy in 1944 and won battles and commendations. At the end of the war, Vargas was ousted in a coup, but he returned in triumph in the election of 1950. Most felt he was less effective as a democratically elected leader than he had been as a dictator, and unrest returned to the country. With a hint of civil war in the wind and the loss of support among the military, Vargas committed suicide in the presidential palace in Rio in 1954. Historians have not yet decided what to make of Vargas, who remains a controversial figure in Brazil. This ambivalence notwithstanding, the widest street in Rio is named in his honour.

Visionary Scheme

President Juscelino Kubitschek dealt Rio what might have seemed a heavy blow. To balance the political and economic influence of Rio and São Paulo, he built Brasília, mobilising the nation to transform a dusty plateau some 960km (600 miles) northwest of Rio into a working capital. Moving the government to the interior had long been under study, but Kubitschek made the world's most ambitious city-planning scheme a reality in just four years. In 1960 Brasília officially became the capital, stripping Rio of almost two centuries of political power.

But Rio refused to wither away. When most diplomats and federal officials eventually and reluctantly accepted their transfers from beachfront to boondocks, their desks were miraculously filled by new legions of bureaucrats. Having lost the political crown to Brasília and the title of biggest and richest city to São Paulo, Rio still managed to prosper.

In 1992, Rio recaptured its political prominence. For one brief, memorable week it hosted the United Nations Conference on Environment and Development, better known as the Earth Summit or simply Rio 92. The conference brought to Rio the largest gathering of world leaders the planet had seen.

Looking to the future

For a while, in the 1980s and 1990s, it seemed that the city might have lost some of its sheen, but Rio today seems fully capable of reinvigorating itself while reaffirming its dedication to the good life. In 2007, Rio hosted the Pan American Games, an excuse to spruce up much of the city's infrastructure, and in 2014 it will be one of the host cities of the FIFA World Cup.

Historical Landmarks

1494 Treaty of Tordesillas divides the New World between Spain and Portugal; Portugal receives territory that will become Brazil.

1500 Pedro Álvares Cabral discovers Brazil.

1502 Rio de Janeiro discovered by Europeans.

1555 French establish colony in Guanabara Bay.

1567 Mem de Sá expels the French; Rio de Janeiro is founded.

1718 Discovery of gold in Minas Gerais.

1763 Capital transferred from Salvador da Bahia to Rio de Janeiro.

1808 Portuguese court moves to Brazil and sets up in Rio.

1822 Brazilian independence declared by Prince Pedro.

1889 Emperor is dethroned by the army; the republic is declared.

1930 Getúlio Vargas takes power after a revolution.

1931 Statue of Christ the Redeemer is inaugurated.

1937 Vargas creates Estado Nôvo, a populist dictatorship.

1954 Vargas commits suicide in the presidential palace.

1960 Capital transferred from Rio de Janeiro to Brasília.

1964 Military coup overthrows president João Goulart.

1967 A new constitution is drawn up; General Artur da Costa e Silva is inaugurated as president.

1968 A military coup closes Congress and gives Costa e Silva dictatorial powers; another, revised constitution is promulgated.

1974 Economic miracle fails; foreign debt soars.

1979 Amnesty issued to all who had been persecuted by military.

1985 Military regime steps down; democracy is restored.

1989 Fernando Collor de Melo elected in direct presidential elections.

1992 Rio de Janeiro hosts Rio 92 (United Nations Conference on Environment and Development).

1994 Real Plan (and new currency) introduced to tame inflation.

2002 Luiz Inácio Lula da Silva ('Lula') elected president.

2007 Rio hosts the Pan American Games. The Christ the Redeemer statue is voted one of the New Seven Wonders of the World in a global poll.

2014 Brazil to host the FIFA World Cup.

WHERE TO GO

Don't expect to see postcard Rio on your way in from the international airport. From the window of your taxi or *frescão* (air-conditioned bus), you'll see only the northern zone's heavy industry and some of the city's shantytowns, the *favelas*. Suddenly, though, you will get your first glimpse of Corcovado and the city will turn all its charms on you.

Most visitors head directly to the Zona Sul, the southern zone. This is the oceanfront area of upper-middle-class suburbs, tourist hotels and the fabled *carioca* beaches of Copacabana, Ipanema, Leblon, São Conrado and Barra da Tijuca where tourists and Rio's elite spend most of their time. Although the suburbs of São Conrado and Barra da Tijuca are more west than south of central Rio, they are still considered to be part of the southern zone. Beyond Barra is the Zona Oeste (western zone), a series of beach communities along the beginning of the coastal road, the Costa Verde highway.

The Centro Histórico, the historic centre, is a busy mixture of colonial and turn-of-the century buildings overshadowed by modern, high-rise office blocks. The charming Santa Teresa district, an inner suburb on a hill within the central area, has superb views of the city and sea; its historic houses, many of which now offer bed-and-breakfast accommodation, give a glimpse of turn-of-the-20th-century Rio. The suburbs of Glória, Catete, Flamengo and Botafogo are graced with sweeping gardens and man-made beaches fronting Guanabara Bay. Tunnels through Rio's several hills link the centre and these suburbs with the Zona Sul.

Extending to the west and north of central Rio is the Zona Norte (northern zone), which, except for Maracanã, the Sambódromo, and perhaps the zoo, is beyond the reach and interest of most foreign visitors.

Cable car up Sugar Loaf

PANORAMIC RIO

No city offers better perches from which to view its splendours. From high atop Sugar Loaf and Corcovado, you'll be rewarded with views of the gods.

Sugar Loaf

From the summit of **Sugar Loaf** (Pão de Açúcar), 396m (1,300ft) above sea level, you can read much of Rio like a map. The cone-shaped peak reportedly earned its name from the first Portuguese settlers, who compared it to mounds of raw sugar.

The simplest way to reach the top of Sugar Loaf is aboard an aerial cable car, which makes the journey in two stages. The trip begins at the Estação Teleférico near Praia Vermelha (Red Beach). All the buses marked 'Urca' pass within a couple of blocks of the station. The first stage of the itinerary takes you to the top of Morro da Urca, at 220m (720ft) somewhat more than half the height of Sugar Loaf. At this way station, which also has good panoramas over Rio, there's a gastronomic centre opened in 2007 and shops, and on most Friday and Saturday evenings at 11.30pm, shows from some of the top Brazilian musical acts. The next car leaves for the Sugar Loaf summit, where you get an airline pilot's view of Botafogo and Guanabara Bay across to Niterói. In fact, you get a pilot's view of the runway at the Santos Dumont airport. There are several *mirantes* (observation points) overlooking Rio, but none more dramatic than this one especially at sunset, when city lights flicker on just across the bay and the flood beams focus on the Christ statue on Corcovado. Take a map with you to help identify landmarks below.

Over all, travel time on the cable cars is only six minutes, with departures at least every 30 minutes from 8.10am to 9pm and much more frequently during busy periods as the cars depart as soon as they are full. Delays rarely occur, but if there's a sudden storm, officials may temporarily suspend traffic, stranding passengers at all levels (but not in mid-air).

Scaling Sugar Loaf

The first person credited with climbing to the summit of Sugar Loaf was a British nanny called Henrietta Carstairs. She made her climb in 1817. Today, if you are fit enough, it is possible to climb the west face in around four to five hours. If you do climb to the top, the cable car down is free.

Corcovado

At 710m (2,326ft), **Corcovado** (open: daily 9am–7pm) – which means 'Hunchback Mountain' – is nearly twice as high as Sugar Loaf and no less a symbol of Rio. The statue of **Cristo Redentor** (Christ the Redeemer), with arms outstretched over the bay, was dedicated as a national monument in 1931, nearly 50 years after the railway reached the summit. The reinforced-

Cristo Redentor

concrete statue, designed by the French sculptor Paul Landowski, is 30m (98ft) tall; a small chapel is built into its base. The statue is covered with an overlay of soapstone and is illuminated by special lamps at night. At any time of day or night you can see the imposing figure from many points of the city. In 2007, it was voted one of the New Seven Wonders of the World in a global poll.

You can arrange for a round-trip taxi to Corcovado, but the most enjoyable means is aboard the funicular, which begins its ascent in Cosme Velho. All buses marked 'Cosme Velho' stop within a few steps of the funicular terminal (Estrada de Ferro Corcovado, Rua Cosme Velho, 513). In 1979 a Swiss cable railway replaced the electrical and steam line opened by Emperor Pedro II in 1884. The trip, which is taken by over 300,000 visitors each year, takes about 20 minutes and passes at a 30-degree angle through full-fledged jungle and rainforest with brilliant flowering trees. The cog trains leave daily every 30 minutes from 8.30am to 6.30pm.

Across from the Cosme Velho station is the **Largo do Boticário** (Apothecary's Square), a small plaza with a colourful collection of (reconstructed) colonial buildings. Just up the street is the **Museu Internacional de Arte Naïf do Brasil, mian** (International Naïve Art Museum of Brazil; Rua Cosme Velho, 561; tel: 2205-8612; open: Tues–Fri 10am–6pm; Sat–Sun and holidays noon–6pm; <www.museunaif.com.br>). Housed in a colonial mansion, the former home of the painter

Eliseu Visconti, and inaugurated in 1995, this collection of naïve art (sometimes called primitive art) is reputed to be the world's biggest and most complete of its kind. Comprising some 8,000 works by Brazilian artists and contributions from 130 countries, the collection includes a painting from Iran that dates from 1327. The immense and colourful painting of Rio you see upon entering, *Rio de Janeiro, Gosto de Você (Rio, I Like You)*, by Lia Mittarakis, is said to be the largest naïve work in the world. It was formerly housed in the Paço Imperial in the city centre, and when it was moved to this location the artist added the MIAN to the bottom of the painting. The museum has a gift shop with some affordable canvases for sale.

Parque Nacional da Tijuca

Corcovado lies within the **Parque Nacional da Tijuca** (Tijuca National Park), a precious jungle wilderness within Rio's city limits. It is the largest forested urban national park in the world and provides a welcome relief from the heat. It has been reforested, because much of Tijuca had been cleared for coffee cultivation in the late 18th century. Tucked within the thick canopy of rainforest is the Cascatinha Táunay, a lovely waterfall; Capela Mayrink, a small, brightly-coloured, 19th-century chapel with much-admired

Wildlife in Tijuca

religious paintings; and the Os Esquilos restaurant (tel: 2492-2197; open: Tues–Sun noon–6pm) a rustic 60-year-old restaurant located in a house dating from 1850. The park has more waterfalls, caves and lookouts including the Mesa do Imperador (The Emperor's Table), where the imperial family used to picnic. Tijuca's network of trails is ideal for hiking. One of the best is the Pico da Tijuca, at just over 1,000m (3,300ft). The trek along the main road and footpath off to the right after Bom Retiro should take about six hours. Other paths require a guide. Excursion companies run half-day bus and jeep tours of the park and its best-known peak, Corcovado. Or you can ask a taxi driver to show you the highlights of this enormous forest, but make sure you fix a price before you leave.

THE ZONA SUL: BEACHES AND MORE

Rio's urban beaches, particularly those in the Zona Sul, are a primary attraction, and an essential element of *carioca* life. But the area is worth exploring for more than its sand. Each of the *bairros* (suburbs, pronounced 'bye-hoos') is distinct, functioning like a small city within a city, with lovely streets, fine restaurants, cosy bars and shopping attractions.

Copacabana and Ipanema are not only Rio's most famous beaches; they are two of the most fabled anywhere. Together they cover more than 6km (4 miles) of glamorous sandy coast, lit by giant flood-lamps (under which you'll see night games of football) and heavily patrolled by tourist police. But Rio has many more beaches to choose from – intimate or expansive, crowded or calm, with or without waves – and all are open to the public without restriction or charge.

Dental floss

When the original thong bikini first appeared on the beaches of Rio, its name could not have described it better: *fio dental* – dental floss.

The great arc of Copacabana Beach

Regardless of where you are staying, for the price of a lemonade you can ride a bus that hugs the coast for 32km (20 miles) or more, travelling in your swimsuit like the *cariocas* and hopping off when you see the beach of your dreams. Here's a rundown of the major beaches and the neighbourhoods attached to them, starting with the southern strand facing the Atlantic and moving west along the most popular of Rio's oceanfront areas. *Cariocas* give thought not only to which beach to go to, but where on that beach to drop their towel. Lifeguard stations, positioned about a kilometre apart from each other, are called *postos*; thus points on the beach are known, for example, as Posto 5 or Posto 9. Certain *postos* are known as hangouts for select groups of people – hipsters, gay people, families, etc. Several of the top hotels in the southern zone provide security for the beaches directly in front of their properties; these are the safest places in town to sunbathe.

Leme is the first beach after the Túnel Novo (New Tunnel), cut through the Morro da Babilônia in 1904 to connect the end of Botafogo to the Atlantic coast. The beginning of Zona Sul's most popular beaches, Leme (Posto 1) is actually the name of the first kilometre of Copacabana Beach. The landmark Iberostar Hotel (previously Le Méridien) is here, just under the shadow of the Morro do Leme, a focal point for the New Year celebrations.

Copacabana

Copacabana, which runs all the way to Posto 6, where small fishing boats are beached, caught the world's imagination long ago. A massive reclamation project extended the beach far out to sea and widened the oceanside avenue and pedestrian areas. The beachside walkway along **Avenida Atlântica** – paved with undulating black-and-white stones, designed by the famous landscape artist Burle Marx, is wide enough for strollers, dog walkers and sightseers. A two-lane path, crowded with joggers, skaters and cyclists, runs alongside. On the landward side of the avenue, pavement cafés at crucial intervals supply *cariocas* with *chopp* (pronounced '*show*-pee', ice-cold draught beer) and *agua de coco* (coconut water).

Strolling along Avenida Atlântica

Once exclusive and chic, Copacabana is today a little worn around the edges as many of the more affluent residents have moved along the coast to Ipanema, Leblon and, more recently, Barra da Tijuca. Prostitutes of all persuasions prowl the hotel zone of Avenida Atlântica after dark, and under-age piranhas pick up solo tourists at the fa-

Fishermen still work from Copacabana

mous disco called Help (pronounced 'helpy'). But Copa is still the primary address of hotels, and its perfect half-moon sands remain a great draw for *cariocas* and tourists alike.

As families sold up their mansions and moved on down the coast, Avenida Atlântica became devoted to expensive high-rise apartment houses and hotels. Many of these buildings have restaurants on the ground floor, usually with open fronts facing the ocean and outdoor tables under sun umbrellas. Apart from little street stalls set up at night selling bikinis, leather goods and Brazilian souvenirs, the main shopping street is one block inland, Avenida Nossa Senhora de Copacabana.

The **Forte de Copacabana** (Copacabana Fort; open: Tues–Sun 10am–5pm), built in 1914 and the scene of a famous military uprising in 1922, lies at the end of the beach in front of the Sofitel Rio Hotel. The peninsula separating Copacabana from Ipanema ends in a rocky outcrop called **Ponta do Arpoador** from which hunters used to harpoon whales.

View of Ipanema from Ponta do Arpoador

Ipanema

On the west side of this outpost lies **Ipanema**. A hilly municipal park named **Praça Garota de Ipanema** (Girl from Ipanema Plaza) honours the bossa nova standard. You'll see plenty
of beautiful girls on the 2-km (1¼-mile) long beach, but Ipanema is also a suburb of elegant apartment houses. Considered
to be more fashionable than Copacabana, Ipanema is less built
up and its beach is cleaner. On Sundays and holidays, the avenue closest to the beach is closed to traffic but open to cyclists
and skaters. One of Ipanema's most fashionable spots is Posto
5, the stretch of beach in front of Rua Vinícius de Morães. Inland along the streets of Ipanema are the most chic fashion boutiques in all of Rio. Ipanema is also home to many of Rio's
favourite bars and restaurants, brimming with atmosphere
and loyal clients. One such place, at the corner of Vinícius de
Morães and Prudente de Morais, is Garota de Ipanema, where
Ipanema's theme song was written in the 1960s.

Leblon and the Botanical Garden

Leblon, the extension of Ipanema, is a wide, relaxed beach and residential neighbourhood with a host of excellent restaurants and *botequims* (bar/restaurants) and Shopping Leblon, arguably the city's most stylish mall. It is divided from its bigger and more famous sister by a canal flanked by gardens with the evocative name of Jardim de Alá (Garden of Allah). The waterway joins the sea with Rio's lagoon, **Lagoa Rodrigo de Freitas**. Even if Rio had no ocean, no bay, no Sugar Loaf, the skyline as seen from the lagoon alone would make it a thoroughly enticing city. Surrounded by parks and luxury urban developments, the lagoon is large enough for motorboat races and calm enough for pedal boats. Along its shore are a jogging path, restaurants, nightclubs and sports grounds. In December a giant Christmas tree floats spectacularly on the water.

Nestled between the lagoon and Corcovado are the **Hípodromo do Jockey Club** and the **Jardim Botânico** (Botanical Garden; open: daily 8am–5pm). This delightfully fragrant enclave on Rua Jardim Botânico, the busy avenue that connects the Leblon and Botafogo districts, occupies 149 hectares (368 acres) and contains more than 7,000 species of tropical plants and trees and at least 140 species of birds. Dom João VI, then prince regent, founded the garden in 1808 in the grounds of a sugar plantation and mill dating back to 1596. The garden is best appreciated on weekday mornings when it is at its quietest.

Beyond the Botanical Garden, just before the Dois Irmãos tunnel, is the en-

Botanical Garden

trance to the quiet **Parque da Cidade** (City Park). Formerly the Morro Queimado coffee plantation, it consists of more
than 160,000 sq m (525,000 sq ft) of gardens and forest reserve. The 19th-century manor house has become the **Museu
Histórico da Cidade** (City Museum; open: Tues–Fri 10am–
4pm, Sat–Sun 10am–3pm), with 17,000 pieces depicting
Rio's development from its founding to the present.

After Leblon the coast road, Avenida Niemeyer, twists
along the rugged side of **Pedra Dois Irmãos** (Two Brothers
Rock), named for its twin peaks. Part of the hillside, which
rises to an altitude of 457m (1,500ft), is occupied by the Vidigal *favela*. Below is **Vidigal** beach, a pretty 550-m (600-yd)
long stretch of sand that is almost the private preserve of the
Sheraton Rio Hotel and Towers.

São Conrado, a beach almost 2km (1.2 miles) long,
begins opposite the decaying shell of the giant, cylindrical
former Hotel National. Bathers here should swim with caution because of the strong tides. São Conrado has three

Rio's Crowded Hillsides

The first *favela* (shantytown) in the history of Rio de Janeiro sprang up
in 1895. Ironically, it was called Providence and was located close to what
is now the British Cemetery at Gamboa in central Rio. Since then, rash-
es of tin-and-plywood shacks have spread to unclaimed hillsides all over
town as poor families, mostly from the northeast of Brazil, flock to Rio
seeking their fortune. If the scattered *favelas* of Rio were considered as
one community, the more than three million inhabitants would form
Brazil's third-largest city. It was made more famous, or perhaps infamous,
by the film *Cidade de Deus* (*City of God*); tourists are advised not to enter
favelas unaccompanied. Visitors who want to see a *favela* should do so
as part of an organised tour. The best is Favela Tours organised by Marcelo Armstrong (tel: 3322-2727; <www.favelatour.com.br>).

Rocinha *favela*

exclusive properties, the Fashion Mall, the Gávea Golf Club and the Inter-Continental Rio. Exclusive as they are, they're just a stone's throw from Rio's largest and most famous *favela*, **Rocinha**, which climbs **Pedra da Gávea**.

Barra da Tijuca

Some elaborate engineering, including double-deck tunnels and viaducts, carries the westward highway along and through the precipitous hillsides to **Barra da Tijuca**, Rio's most modern and rapidly developing suburb. Backed by lagoons, this is by far Rio's longest beach: 18km (11 miles) of sand that seem to stretch to infinity – but beware of dangerous ocean currents, large waves and constant Atlantic winds, conditions that bring out the surfers and wind-surfers by the dozens. The area is noted for its seafood and *churrascaria* (barbecue) restaurants, its shopping and entertainment centres and chic beach-goers.

Sitio Burle Marx

Beyond the Zona Sul

The first beach after Barra is **Recreio dos Bandeirantes**, a 1.5-km (1-mile) long beach with rough seas. Recreio is the next target for development after Barra. Strong surf limits the possibilities for swimmers, but it enhances them for *surfistas* at the next beach further down, tiny and secluded **Prainha** (Little Beach), set beneath pretty green hills. The most popular beach in this area is **Grumari**, which is located in an ecological sanctuary and has remained relatively unspoilt. The steep hill at the end of Grumari will take you up to **Point da Grumari** (open: 11.30am–6.30pm) where you can dine or drink with spectacular views of the coast below and a magnificent sunset at the end of the day. Don't bother going in search of the beaches you can see from Point da Grumari, however, as they are part of another ecological reserve, access to which is strictly controlled by the army.

At the Grumari end of Barra da Tijuca is the **Sitio Burle Marx** (Estrada da Barra de Guaratiba, 2019; tel: 2410-1412; open: Tues–Sun 9.30am–1.30pm; call in advance to book a tour), the former estate, gardens, botanical laboratory and studio of Brazil's best-known landscape architect. Opened after Roberto Burle Marx's death in 1994 by the Brazilian government, which inherited the estate, this is a place few people seem to know about, but one you should not miss if you have even a single day for an excursion from Rio. A visit here can easily be combined with a day at the beach nearby. In an area of over 40 hectares (100 acres), the estate displays more than 3,500 tropical and semi-tropical plant species, many of them rare; of the several discovered by Burle Marx himself, the most famous is the Sitio's signature flower, the *Heliconia burle marxii*. More than 250 species of palms are found here, including the Ceylon species, which blooms only every 70 years or so. The grounds also feature a Benedictine chapel that dates to 1610; it is still used for Mass and weddings, as it was during the 45 years Burle Marx lived on the property.

Burle Marx created imaginative landscape projects throughout Brazil and abroad, but some of his best-known work is in Rio: the Parque do Flamengo, entirely man-made; the emblematic, undulating tiles along Copacabana beach; and the gardens of the Fine Arts Museum and the National Library, to name but a few. The American Institute of Architects called him 'the real creator of the modern garden'.

Among the other attractions at the westernmost point of Barra da Tijuca is the **Museu Casa do Pontal** (Estrada do Pontal, 3295; tel: 2490-3278; open: Thur–Sun 9.30am–5pm), which has an extensive collection of popular Brazilian art forms. Here, too, is the city's water park, Rio Water Planet (Estrada das Bandeirantes, 24000; tel: 2428-9000; open: 10am–5pm; <www.rio waterplanet.com.br>).

Casa do Pontal exhibit

Paço Imperial

THE CENTRO HISTÓRICO

Around Praça XV de Novembro

Although remnants of colonial architecture are found in many parts of Rio, the greatest concentration of historic monuments is near **Praça XV de Novembro** (15 November Square). Called simply Praça XV (pronounced '*prah*-suh *keen*-zee'), it is the heart of the old city. In 1590, Carmelite fathers constructed a convent on this site. A number of watershed events in Brazilian history transpired here: two emperors were crowned on the spot. The first emperor, Dom Pedro, chose the site to make public his decision to remain in Brazil rather than return to Portugal. Also, the abolition of slavery was proclaimed on Praça XV from the balcony of the Imperial Palace. From 1743 to 1889, when Rio was the capital of Brazil, the square was home to the national government. It was re-christened Praça XV to commemorate the date when the Brazilian republic was declared in 1889.

With your back to the bay, the elegant, three-storey colonial building on your left is the **Paço Imperial** (Imperial Palace; open: Tues–Sun noon–6pm; <www.pacoimperial.com.br>). Completed in 1743, it was once the residence of the Portuguese viceroys. As the city's fortunes rose, the building was pressed into service as the royal (later imperial) palace. In 1985 the fully renovated palace was reinaugurated as a cultural centre. Inside are attractive bars and restaurants, including Atrium del Rey, Bistrô do Paço and Bar das Artes.

Across Rua 1 de Março from the square are two 18th-century churches separated by a narrow passageway. The one on the left, with a tall corner bell tower, is the **Igreja de Nossa Senhora do Carmo** (Carmelite Church; open: Mon–Fri 8am–2pm, Sat 8am–noon), until 1978 the diocesan cathedral. Note the six upstairs balconies where royalty used to sit (commoners, of course, sat below). A plaque in the corridor of the sacristy covers an urn said to have contained the ashes of Cabral, the Portuguese explorer who discovered Brazil for the Europeans in 1500. The baroque interior is modest compared with that of the **Igreja da Ordem Terceira do Monte do Carmo** (open: Mon–Fri 8am–2pm, Sat 8am–noon), next door. Notice the exuberant decorations on the walls, the rich altar, and the marble works of Mestre Valentim, the creator of the Praça XV fountain.

At the far end of the walkway between the two churches, over a gate, stands one of the few public oratories remaining in Rio.

Another historical architectural feature is located on the north side of Praça XV:

Island escape

Taking the walkway at the harbour end of Praça XV brings you to the ferry terminal where boats and hydrofoils sail regularly for Niterói and Paquetá Island.

the **Arco do Teles**, the last colonial arch in Rio. The tiny street that begins at the Arco, **Travessa do Comércio**, is lined by a series of well-preserved, two-storey townhouses. The Brazilian bombshell Carmen Miranda lived at No. 13 as a young girl; her mother owned a modest bar on the street. Today it's a lively spot with bars that spill out onto the cobblestones. On many evenings you'll find impromptu *pagode* (street samba) at one end, and at the other, clubs where bands and disco lights are already pumping at 6pm. The *povão* (masses) hang out at the *pagode*; those intent on making an impression go down the street.

National History Museum

If there is one museum in Rio that should be of interest to the foreign visitor, it is the **Museu Histórico Nacional** (National History Museum; tel: 2550-9224; open: Tues–Fri 10am–5.30pm, Sat–Sun 2–6pm; <www.museuhistoriconacional.com.br>), which covers the history of Brazil from its discovery by Europeans in 1500 to the Proclamation of the Republic in 1889.

Founded in 1922, the museum is located in the historic centre of Rio, close to Praça XV, and can be included in any tour of central Rio. It is housed in the remains of the Santiago Fort, built in 1603, and the old arsenal, the Casa do Trem, built in 1762. The museum contains an archive of more than 287,000 pieces that include armaments, carriages, paintings, photographs, furniture, documents and even the pen used by Princess Isabel to sign the proclamation that effectively abolished slavery. The museum has the largest collection of coins and banknotes in Latin America.

The National History Museum is complimented by the **Museu da República** (Museum of the Republic) in Catete (*see page 56*) which picks up the story of Brazil from just prior to the Proclamation of the Republic until the capital of the country moved to Brasília in 1960.

Cultural Corridor

The area running from Rua 1 de Março and Praça XV to Avenida Presidente Vargas is known as the 'cultural corridor'. Here you'll find the **Centro Cultural Banco do Brasil** (open: Tues–Sun 10am–9pm; <www.bb.com.br>), which hosts a wide range of cultural programmes and exhibitions; the **Casa França-Brasil** (open: Tues–Sun noon–8pm; <www.fcfb.rj.gov.br>) occupying a customs' house dating from

Centro Cultural Banco do Brasil

1820; and the **Espaço Cultural da Marinha** (open: Tues–Sun noon–5pm; <www.mar.mil.br/sdm>), a space dedicated to the history of navigation and the Brazilian navy. It is also possible to cruise the bay from here on the *Laurindo Pitta*, a British tug built in 1910. The cruise, which takes place from Thursday to Sunday at 1.15pm and 3.15pm, includes visits to the Ilhas das Cobras, Ilha Villegaignon and Ilha Fiscal.

Avenida Presidente Vargas starts at Praça Pio X (Pius X Square), which contains the cathedral-sized **Igreja de Nossa Senhora da Candelária** (open: Mon–Fri 8am–4pm; Sat–Sun 9am–1pm). Construction of this sumptuous church, which achieves harmony between its baroque and neoclassical features, began in 1775 and took 123 years to complete. The interior is decorated with marble of remarkably varied colours, and the sacristy boasts gorgeous carvings in jacaranda wood. Thanks to the Avenida Vargas project, which demolished many nearby buildings, the Candelária church now stands in distinguished isolation at a dramatic crossroads.

Although you can't miss the Candelária church, you won't be able to find your way to the **Igreja e Mosteiro de São Bento** (St Bento Church and Monastery; open: daily 7–11am, 2–6pm; <www.osb.org.br>) without knowing a secret. The trick is to walk down Rua Dom Gerardo, slip into an unmarked modern building at number 40, and take the lift to the top floor. The roof of the building leads to the grounds of the church and monastery. (You can also do it the harder way, via the gate at Rua Dom Gerardo, 68 and an uphill walk.) A cool retreat from the city below, São Bento is one of Rio's most valued artistic and historical treasures. Part of a Benedictine monastery, the church was completed in 1641. Its simple, Mannerist façade has twin towers capped with pyramids. Large arched doorways with wrought-iron gates lead to 17th-century portals of finely carved wood. Inside are Portuguese marble floors and a wealth of florid carved and gilded decor, which reaches up to a painted, vaulted ceiling and two heavy chandeliers. Much of the intricate carvings, bathed in red and gold, are the work of the renowned master, Frei Domingos da Conceição.

Inside St Bento

Every Sunday at 10am, a Mass with Gregorian chants is held. Most Saturdays, around 3pm, you're likely to catch a wedding in progress – this is your best chance of seeing the fabulous interior completely illuminated. To visit the monastery adjoining the church, advance permission is required; only men are admitted, except when special processions are held.

Central Rio from Santa Teresa

CENTRAL RIO

There are various worthwhile sights inland from Guanabara Bay, just west of the Historic Centre. The city's main street, **Avenida Rio Branco**, was originally part of a visionary project at the start of the 20th century: a perfectly straight avenue with a row of brazilwood trees down the middle. But the trees and tram tracks ultimately gave way to cars and congestion.

West of Avenida Rio Branco

From the crossroads of avenidas President Vargas and Rio Branco, you can see the biggest clock in town, occupying six floors of the tower above the **Estação Dom Pedro II** (Dom Pedro II Railway Station), better known as Central do Brasil. The station, known for its seedy life and train surfers (those who risk death 'surfing' on top of moving trains), was immortalised in Walter Salles' affecting 1997 film *Central Station*.

Just north of Central, along Rua Bento Ribeiro and Rua Rivadavia Correia, is **Cidade do Samba** (Samba City; tel: 2213-2503; open: Tues–Sat 9am–5pm; <http://cidadedosambarj.globo.com>). Formerly dock warehouses, Cidade do Samba acts as a central staging post for Rio's main samba schools. Depending on the time of year visitors can see either floats and costumes from the previous Carnaval, or the new floats and costumes being made for the upcoming celebrations. There is usually a special Carnaval show on Thursday nights at 9pm.

Next to the Praça São Caetano, in Rua Luis de Camoes, is the **Real Gabinete Português de Leitura** (Royal Portuguese Reading Room; open: Mon–Fri 9am–6pm), a library of quiet, stunning beauty. Built in 1837 and restored in 1997, Rio's Reading Room features three levels of antique books, carved iron balustrades, an iron chandelier and a massive, stained-glass skylight.

Confeitaria Colombo

In nearby Praça Tiradentes, at No. 79, is the famed **Gafieira Estudantina** (tel: 2232-1149), a dimly lit dance hall that evokes 1930s Brazil. Even if you don't like dancing, the popular and casual Estudantina may change your mind. Open Thursday to Saturday from 10pm, things begin to roll about midnight.

In Rua Gonçalves Dias, at No. 32, is the much-photographed **Confeitaria Colombo** (open: Mon–Fri 9am–

8pm, Sat 9.30am–5pm; <www.confeitariacolombo.com.br>). Rio's most historic café, which first opened in 1894, is another spot of classic *carioca* flavour and ideal for taking a break. It stops the clock with its elegant belle époque decor: eight giant Belgian mirrors, with hand-carved jacaranda frames, and Louis XV-style furnishings. A paradise for lovers of sweets, Colombo offers an indulgent lunch and afternoon tea. It also operates the Café do Forte within the Forte do Copacabana (tel: 3201-4049; open: Tues–Sun 10am–8pm).

Rua Gonçalves Dias runs into **Largo da Carioca**, a small park that was once a lagoon. The installation of a Metrô station here has created a rather austere landscape, except for the permanent street vendors, or *camellões*. Nothing has changed on the promontory above, which is occupied by two colonial-era churches. The **Igreja e Convento de Santo Antônio** (Church and Convent of St Anthony; open: Mon–Fri 7.30am–6pm), on the left, was founded at the beginning of the 17th century. St Anthony is an exceedingly popular saint in Rio, as in his native Lisbon, so the church is often packed. On 13 June, the saint's feast day – he's known as Santo Antônio Casamenteiro, the marrying saint – unmarried women come to pay their respects and pray for a husband. A lift inside the hill saves some of the visitors climbing steps.

The church next door to Santo Antônio has the lofty title **Igreja da Venerável Ordem Terceira de São Francisco da Penitência** (Church of the Venerable Third Order of St Francis of the Penitence; open: Tues–Fri 9am–noon, 1–4pm). Known simply as São Francisco and built between 1622 and 1738, the beautiful 18th-century interior is extremely ornate: a veritable treasure house of distinguished baroque workmanship in wood, gilt and marble. As you enter the church, notice the moustachioed saints on each side.

Architecture critics and common citizens disagree about the new **Metropolitan Cathedral** (open: 6am–7pm; <www.

catedral.com.br>), also called Catedral Nova, which rises like a volcano on the horizon southwest of Largo da Carioca. Dating from 1964, but not completed until 1979, the design of the reinforced-concrete and glass structure has been described as a truncated cone or an Etruscan pyramid. Huge stained-glass windows flood the interior with light. A sacred art museum (open: Sat–Sun 9–11am and 1–4pm) is located in the basement.

Cinelandia

Avenida Rio Branco abandons commerce for culture in its southernmost few blocks, an area known as Cinelandia for the many movie houses that sprang up there in the 1930s. Each September and October Cinelandia is again the focal point for the Brazilian film industry when the main screenings at the Rio Film Festival (Festival do Rio) take place in the recently restored Cine Odeon, which first opened its doors back in 1926.

The **Theatro Municipal** (tel: 2299-1711; <www.theatro municipal.rj.gov.br>), which dominates Cinelandia, is an opera house that opened in 1909 and is one of Rio's prized architectural and cultural monuments. Its exterior and entrance are copies of the Paris Opera House. Pavlova, Caruso, Toscanini and, more recently, Barishnikov, Pavarotti, Kiri Te Kanawa and Oscar Peterson have all brought international culture to Rio at the Municipal.

Two more neoclassical buildings from the same era complete the ensemble. Across Avenida Rio Branco is the **Museu Nacional de Belas Artes** (National Fine Arts Museum; open: Tues–Fri 10am–6pm, Sat–Sun 2–6pm; <www.mnba.gov.br>), said to be inspired by the Louvre in Paris. It traces the history of Brazilian painting from 18th-century academics to trend-setting modernists. Among those represented are Eliseu Visconti (1867–1944 and Cândido Portinari (1903–62), one of Brazil's pivotal modern painters. Opposite is the **Palácio Pedro Ernesto**, now City Hall, dedicated in 1923. Back across Rio

Branco is the **Biblioteca Nacional** (National Library, open: Mon–Fri 11am–3pm; tel: 2220-9484; visits must be booked in advance). Peek at the stately exterior and entrance – its staircase and stained-glass cupola make it look more like an opera house than a library – but don't waste time trying to see more. The library is run like a high-security repository of state secrets.

Close to Cinelandia is the district known as **Lapa**, a bohemian area with a happening night scene. Here, you can't miss a utilitarian monument that's still standing and functioning, the **Arcos da Lapa** (Lapa Aqueduct). Otherwise called Os Arcos (The Arches), it suggests that the Romans beat the Portuguese to Rio, but it was actually put into operation in 1750. In 1896, when the city's water supply was diverted to more modern channels, the monument became a viaduct for a tram line linking central Rio with the hills of Santa Teresa. Astoundingly, the trams still rattle across the narrow bridge.

Arcos da Lapa

SANTA TERESA

One of the best ways to see Rio as it looked a century ago is to visit the picturesque district of **Santa Teresa**, a hillside inner suburb. Funding has finally arrived to spruce up and show off this bohemian neighbourhood's historic homes, including many that now offer a form of bed-and-breakfast known as Cama e Café (<www.camaecafe.com.br>). A nice walk takes you along the ongoing restoration project ('Colours of Santa Teresa') of colonial and 19th-century homes and shops on Largo do Guimarães and ruas Carlos Magno, Paschoal, Monte Alegro, Áurea, Orientes and Progresso, until you reach Largo das Neves and the Igreja Nossa Senhora das Neves.

There are faster ways of reaching Santa Teresa, but the *bondinho*, Rio's last surviving tram line, is the most fun. Catch the Paula Mattos line at the tram station behind the Petrobrás

Bondinho in Santa Teresa

building (opposite the cathedral). The conductor moves along the running board collecting fares en route; and youngsters leap on and off the moving tram to avoid paying. The tracks twist and turn sharply on the steep hillsides. Watch your belongings on the open-sided cars.

Two side-by-side sights should not be missed in Santa Teresa. One is the enchanting **Museu Chácara do Céu**

Bonde bombshell

The common name for tram, *bonde* – or *bondinho*, the diminutive – comes from a time when the street cars were financed by bonds. One of the first tram companies went belly up, making losers of all those who held shares. So *bonde* became the derisive nickname for the modern trolleys that replaced mule-driven carriages.

(Rua Murtinho Nobre, 93; open: Wed–Mon noon–5pm; <www.museuscastromaya.com.br>). Appropriately named, the 'Little House of Heaven' sits in a manicured garden on a hilltop with fantastic views over Rio. The house and artworks reveal the personality of the entrepreneur and collector, Raymundo Ottoni de Castro Maya, who was one of the founders of the Museum of Modern Art. The permanent collection upstairs is of 18th- and 19th-century landscapes of Rio and Brazil, which capture the New World wonder of life here.

Connected to the museum is **Parque das Ruinas** (Ruins Park; open: Wed–Sun 10am–10pm) inaugurated in 1997. Although it sounds like an archaeological dig, it is an ingeniously rehabilitated mansion. Built as the palace of Joaquim Murtinho Nobre, the mansion was subsequently the home of society dame Laurinda Santos Lobo, who entertained the likes of dancer Isadora Duncan and the Brazilian composer Heitor Villa-Lobos. For decades the mansion sat abandoned on top of the hill. Rather than destroy it or attempt to reconstruct it, the hollowed-out structure was converted into an open-air space for banquets, fashion shows and business events.

BAIRROS SOUTH OF CENTRAL RIO

Four *bairros* (suburbs) – Glória, Catete, Flamengo and Botafogo, hug the Bay of Guanabara. They extend north to south from central Rio, just west of **Parque do Flamengo**. This man-made park, which lies across Botafogo Bay from Sugar Loaf, was part of an urban facelift. In a colossal land-fill programme, completed in 1960, nearly 120 hectares (300 acres) were reclaimed from the harbour for the freeways that link Centro to the Zona Sul proper. Brazil's master landscape architect, Roberto Burle Marx, transformed the new terrain into a green belt between the sea and the city. The park is a popular recreation area, with a number of playing fields and other attractions.

Beaches in Town

With such a surfeit of excellent beaches to the south, those closer to central Rio may seem less appealing. Though they're admittedly not as pretty, they are popular with Brazilians and convenient if you're doing some sightseeing in the Centro Histórico.

Flamengo is the beach closest to the business district and the first to get crowded. This man-made beach forms part of the ambitious Parque do Flamengo project. Harbour waters are gentle but murky. Botafogo is another man-made harbour beach of brilliant white sand. Sharing the cove here are the pleasure boats of the Rio Yacht Club. Urca, barely 100m long and squeezed in under Sugar Loaf, has striking views of the Rio skyline. The beach immediately below, to the left as you ride the cable car up to Morro da Urca, is Praia Vermelha (Red Beach), which has a view of almost uninterrupted hills and islands. Small and close to town, this beach of coarse, dark sand tends to fill up with sunbathers. An attractive *pista*, or path, ideal for strolling or jogging, extends from this beach.

Glória and Flamengo

Curving along the Glória Marina and Flamengo beach, the park tends to fill up at weekends. The most popular sport on the playing fields behind the beach is football; informal matches, often with barefoot players, go on virtually 24 hours a day. Unlike the Rio Yacht Club in Botafogo, with its millionaire membership, the **Marina da Glória** (<www.marinadagloria.com.br>) is open to anyone. Hire boats there for sailing, fishing or for a trip in the bay.

The view of Sugar Loaf from Marina da Glória

Overlooking the park from a bluff that was once right alongside the harbour is a small and simple church so appealing you may want to take the funicular up for a look. The simple, harmonious lines of the **Igreja de Nossa Senhora da Glória do Outeiro** (Gloria Church on the Hill; open: Tues–Fri 8am–5pm, Sat–Sun 9am–noon; <www.outeirodagloria.org.br>) date from 1739. During the 19th century, the imperial family attended Sunday Mass here. Inside, the church's walls are decorated with handsome old Portuguese *azulejos* (blue-and-white decorative tiles), and Mestre Valemtim decorated the wooden altar. The church today is fashionable for weddings.

Flamengo Park contains three museums. From north to south, the first is the **Museu de Arte Moderna** (Modern Art Museum; open: Tues–Fri noon–6pm, Sat–Sun noon–7pm; <www.mamrio.com.br>). A daring architectural scheme in 1948, the structure stands on stilts and is surrounded by richly integrated gardens. In 1978 it suffered a catastrophic fire that spared the structure but devoured a considerable part of the museum's collection. As well as displaying items from the

Carmen Miranda

surviving 4,000 items in its archives, the museum is also a popular location for visiting exhibitions and shows and houses the popular Vivo Rio Showhouse.

The **Museu do Monumento aos Mortos da Segunda Guerra** (Museum of the Monument to the Dead of World War II; open: Tues–Sun 10am–5pm) is part of a monumental ensemble topped by slim, twin pillars that represent two arms raised to beseech God in prayer. Pope John Paul II celebrated mass from the steps in 1980 to a crowd estimated to be of around two million people. On display in the museum are weapons, gas masks, helmets and battle flags that commemorate Brazil's contribution to the campaign against the German army in Italy. The Tomb of the Unknown Soldier is also here.

In a modern, circular building, tucked away in the trees of Flamengo Park, is **Museu Carmen Miranda** (open: Tues–Fri 11am–5pm, Sat–Sun 2–5pm; <www.carmenmiranda.net>), where fans of the late Brazilian Bombshell (who was actually born in Portugal) can view 1,500 items, comprising jewellery, photos and her costumes, including those trippy hats and shoes.

Catete

Running almost parallel inland from Flamengo Park is the *bairro* of Catete. Here you'll find Catete Palace, which houses the fine **Museu da República** (Museum of the Republic; open: Tues–Fri noon–5pm, Sat–Sun 2–6pm; <www.museuda

republica.org.br>). This regal palace served as the official residence of Brazil's presidents from 1897 to 1954 – until President Getúlio Vargas killed himself in his third-floor bedroom here. In 1960, when the seat of the national government was transferred to the new city of Brasília, the palace became a museum. The spectacular, mid-19th-century residence is a paean to New World wealth, Rio's very own Versailles. It was built by a coffee baron, the Barão de Nova Friburgo, who went broke after sinking his entire fortune into the mansion. The Second Empire decorations and furnishings, floors, ceilings, walls, mirrors and chandeliers are so stunning that they upstage the exhibits upstairs that recount the history of the republic. Those with an interest in the macabre side of Brazilian history, however, will want to see the glass-enclosed display of the very pajamas Vargas was wearing when he pointed a gun to his chest (the neat bullet hole and small blood stain are intact).

Museu da República

A few doors down, at Rua do Catete, 181, is the handsomely designed and instructive **Museu do Folclore Edison Carneiro** (open: Tues–Fri 11am–6pm, Sat–Sun 3–6pm; <www.museudo folclore.com.br>). This folklore museum houses an excellent collection of popular art, crafts and items used in regional rites and rituals, such as Catholic ex-votos, Candomblé *orixás* (gods or spirits) and Carnaval costumes. The 1,000 items on display provide a superb introduction to Brazilian popular culture.

Botafogo

The suburb of Botafogo, which joins Flamengo to the lagoon, has two small museums that offer intriguing looks at Brazilian culture. The **Museu do Índio** (Indian Museum; Rua das Palmeiras, 55; open: Tues–Fri 9am–5.30pm, Sat–Sun 1–5pm; <www.museudoindio.org.br>), operated by the national Indian foundation, FUNAI, has appealing ceramics in unusual colours, headdresses of all ranks, dolls and musical instruments, and a huge drum for long-distance calls. For visitors with an interest in music, **Museu Villa-Lobos** (Rua Sorocaba, 200; open; Mon–Fri 10am–5.30pm; <www.museuvillalobos.org. br>) is dedicated to the Brazilian classical composer, celebrated for incorporating the sounds of Brazilian popular culture into his music, such as in the series Bachianas Brasileiras.

GUANABARA BAY

Rio's picturesque, if polluted, harbour has an area of about 250 sq km (160 sq miles), room enough for warships, ferries, yachts and dozens of islands and inlets. To cross from Rio to Niterói you can take the cheapest commuter ferry in town or a high-flying hydrofoil. Or ride on a bus or drive a car across the six-lane toll bridge that marches across the bay on heavy stilts. The bridge, opened in 1974, is 13½km (8½ miles) long; the height in the middle of the bay is high enough to let any ship pass.

Leaving the **Estação das Barcas** (Boat Station) close to Praça XV is fascinating. To your right (starboard side) is the main runway of Rio's in-town airport, Santos Dumont. To your left (port side) is a small island called **Ilha Fiscal** (open for tours Thur–Sun at 1, 2.30 and 4pm). The green fortress with bizarre towers in Arabian Nights style was opened in 1889. It was here that the last ball of the Empire was held on 19 February 1889, exactly nine months to the day before the Republic was proclaimed and Emperor Pedro II was forced to abdicate.

Niterói

Niterói, until 1975 the capital of the state of Rio de Janeiro, is really quite provincial and was once the base for a section of the British community. From here there are spectacular views back towards Rio; a great place to take in the sights is from the veranda of the acclaimed **Museu de Arte Contemporânea**

Museu de Arte Contemporânea

Niterói's organ

Niterói is home to the largest tube organ in Latin America and one of only 10 in the world designed to perform Bach's Fugues. Built in 1956, the organ, of Italian origin, can be found in the Basilica of Nossa Senhora Auxiliadora on Rua Santa Rosa.

(open: Tues–Sun 10am–6pm), which occupies a promontory overlooking Praia da Boa Viagem. Opened in 1996, it contains Brasilian artworks. But most distinctive is the building itself: designed by Oscar Niemeyer, from a distance it resembles a gigantic flying saucer.

On the Niterói side of the bay, but some way from the town, is the **Fortaleza de Santa Cruz** (Fort of Santa Cruz; open: Tues–Fri noon–5pm, Sat–Sun 9am–5pm), parts of which date back to the 17th century. Guarding the entrance to the bay, Santa Cruz is considered to be, architecturally speaking, Brazil's most important historic fortification.

Deep in the bay, just over an hour's ferry ride from Rio, but still leaving from the Estação das Barcas, lies a lush green island of utter tranquillity. **Ilha da Paquetá** enjoys a total lack of cars; the only motorised vehicles are a very few delivery vans and an ambulance. To get around the mostly unpaved roads of the island, residents and tourists rely on bicycles, horse-drawn carriages and a so-called bus – actually a tractor-powered 'train' on rubber tyres. The island's area is about 110 hectares (270 acres); you can see it all on foot in half a day.

THE COSTA VERDE

Beyond Barra and the outer beaches of Rio, Highway BR 101 wends gently along the mountainous Costa Verde, or Green Coast. It delights with amazing views of brilliant bays and striking promontories, deserted beaches, lush tropical vegetation and mist-covered islands stretching out into the Atlantic Ocean. The road will take you all the way to the state of São Paulo and is the most picturesque way to drive between the cities of Rio de Janeiro and São Paulo.

Angra dos Reis

It's tempting to say that the Costa Verde is south of Rio, since it is further down the Brazilian coastline, but it is actually due west. There are attractive stops all along the coast, but the first major destination, about two hours (150km/94 miles) from Rio, is **Angra dos Reis**. An ugly little jumble of a town by itself, Angra sits on a spectacular series of eight bays with 360 islands. Over 80 percent of the municipal area of Angra is protected by environmental laws. A boat cruise in the bay is essential – and nearer to Rio a trip around some of the tropical islands can be made from the port of Itacuruçá (68km/42 miles)

Angra dos Reis

Snorkelling off the Costa Verde

– but one of the prime attractions is **Ilha Grande** (Big Island; <www.ilha grande.com.br>), a two-hour ferry ride from Angra. Ilha Grande Is the kind of place, with abundant sun, natural vegetation, gorgeous beaches and equally handsome people that reduces one to clichés about tropical idylls. The island is draped in Atlantic forest, reaches a height of 1,040m (3,410ft), and has more than 160km (100 miles) of shoreline (including more than 100 beaches, many of them absolutely deserted). Pirates used to hang out here. Today it's mostly weekenders from São Paulo and Rio and foreigners in search of eco-paradise.

The main town on the sparsely developed island is **Vila do Abraão**, where the ferry from Angra docks. It's a cute town with a little green-and-white church, numerous relaxed *pousadas* (inns) to stay at, and beachfront seafood restaurants.

Still, your best bet here is to explore the island's natural wonders. Take a schooner cruise around it and the bay, or stroll to the quiet little beach of **Abraãozinho**. Better yet, a $2-million sustainable development project, partly funded by the World Bank, is protecting and connecting a series of 16 trails totalling 110km (68 miles). A recommended hike, which takes about two hours, is to the far side of the island and the beautiful beach of **Lopes Mendes**, often voted as one of the world's best.

Paraty

For those interested in living history, **Paraty** may be paradise. A perfectly preserved colonial gem, Paraty (also spelt Parati, and recognised by UNESCO as one of the most important surviving examples of colonial architecture) is a tiny square of uneven stone streets, colonial churches and squat white houses with brightly coloured doors and windows. The entire old town is pedestrians-only. Founded in 1667, Paraty is a further 100km (60 miles) down the coast from Angra, or about four hours from Rio. In the 17th and 18th centuries, Paraty was the second most important port in Brazil and a central element of the Caminho do Ouro (Gold Trail), also known as the Estrada Real or Royal Road. Gold and precious gemstones from Minas Gerais were shipped to Europe out of Paraty. When roads and later rail to Rio were built, Paraty's importance waned. But because of its early decline, it escaped further construction and modernisation and exists in a colonial time warp. The town has been declared a national historic monument.

Paraty is an ideal place to wander idly, except for the fact that the streets' irregularly shaped and placed stones, called *pé-de-moleque*, may have you looking at your feet as much as the houses. The highlights include the colonial churches. **Santa Rita**, founded in 1722, faces the port and serves as the unofficial postcard of Paraty. It houses a small museum of religious art; next to it is the **Casa da Cadéia**, the old prison, in operation until 1980. The original **Matriz de Nossa Senhora dos Remédios**, built in 1646, even pre-

Latin literature

Since 2003, Paraty has hosted Brazil's most important and prestigious literary festival, a five-day tropical version of Britain's Hay-on-Wye. Conceived by the British publisher, Liz Calder, who has a house in the village, the July festival attracts top literary names from all over Latin America and further afield (<www.flip.org.br>).

dated the town. The present neoclassical structure, literally left-leaning, was begun in 1712. The **Capela de Nossa Senhora das Dores** (Chapel of Our Lady of Pain), built in 1800, faces the Baía de Paraty. The sober and elegant **Igreja de Nossa Senhora de Rosário** (Our Lady of the Rosary), on Rua do Comércio, was built in 1725 by slaves.

Paraty has moonlighted as a set for films depicting historic Brazil. *Gabriela*, based on the Jorge Amado novel and starring Sônia Braga and Marcello Mastroanni, was filmed here, as were segments of *Kiss of the Spider Woman*, while beaches close to Paraty were used for the 2006 horror flick *Turistas*.

Paraty has been discovered by tourists, but amazingly it remains a quiet village where people still live and work, primarily as fishermen or guides on schooner cruises. In bars at night, you'll mix with locals dancing *forró* and samba, as well as with tourists from all over the world. Given the distance from Rio, it is certainly worth spending one or more nights in the inns of Paraty, of which there are more than 80. One inn, the Pousada de Principe, is run by the descendants of the last Emperor.

Buses leave for Angra dos Reis and Paraty from the Novo Rio Rodoviária, but given the outstanding beauty of the region, this could be the time to hire a car.

INLAND FROM RIO

In January and February, when the sun begins to melt the asphalt streets of Rio, well-to-do *cariocas* head for the hills, to the relatively cool climate of the Serra dos Órgãos (Organ Mountains). This has been the fashionable thing to do since the days of Emperor Pedro II, who built his summer palace here and had the town of Petrópolis named after him. When Pedro moved up to Petrópolis in the summer months, he was generally followed by the foreign ambassadors who also established summer residences.

Petrópolis

Petrópolis is only about 65km (40 miles) from the centre of
Rio; after the heavy traffic of northern Rio's grim industrial
outskirts, the scenery becomes a wonder of tropical colour:
hibiscus, bougainvillaea and orchids. The roads are lined
with banana sellers lying in wait.

Known as the *cidade imperial* (imperial city), Petrópolis
sits at an altitude of 900m (2,950ft); while that guarantees
a measure of relief from the sea-level heat, the German- and
Swiss-style chalets of the area seem a bit of an exaggeration.
Part fantasy, they are testimony to the homesickness of the
early colonists, many of whom were German.

Excursion companies in Rio run half-day and full-day
tours to Petrópolis; you can also drive (allow about two
hours each way) or take one of the frequent express buses
from Novo Rio bus station. The nicest way to tour the streets

En route to Petrópolis

and squares of Petrópolis is by horse-and-carriage, which gives you ample time to appreciate the old villas and their gardens. It's also a delightful city for walking.

However you travel, try to plan your visit in harmony with the schedule of the **Museu Imperial** (open: Tues–Sun 11am–6pm; <www.museuimperial.gov.br>). Opened in 1945, the museum is housed in the neoclassical Summer Palace, built exactly one century earlier. Noteworthy paintings, tapestries and furniture fill the building; the floors are so fine that visitors are required to don soft overshoes. The most valuable single exhibit, kept under armed guard, is the imperial crown of Pedro II. Studded with 639 diamonds and 77 pearls, it weighs more than 1.5kg (3lb).

São Pedro Cathedral

During the 20th century, Petrópolis became the summer residence of the president of the republic. Only opened to the public in 1997, **Palácio Rio Negro** (open: Wed–Sun 9.30am–5pm, Mon noon–5pm) was the palace where Getúlio Vargas and Juscelino Kubitschek, among other presidents, spent quite a bit of time before Rio de Janeiro lost its status as capital of Brazil. The yellow palace originally belonged to the Barão de Rio Negro, a coffee baron of the late 19th century. The residence, in spectacular shape, is perhaps most notable for the stunning, original parquet floors of varied Brazilian woods. The hardwood motifs change from room to room. Note also the huge bathrooms.

Catedral São Pedro de Alcântara (open: daily 8am–noon, 2–6pm) looks ancient and a mite out of place in Brazil, but it's a case of late 19th-century architects looking back with admiration on French Gothic churches; although the first stone was laid by the emperor in 1884, it wasn't completed until 1939. Behind a wrought-iron fence are the tombs of Emperor Pedro II and the royal family. Starting at the cathedral is **Avenida Koeler**, lined with handsomely restored aristocratic mansions, which include the aforementioned Palácio Rio Negro.

The meticulously restored **Palácio de Cristal**, reopened in 1998, is a crystal palace built in France in 1879. It was a gift from the Conde d'Eu to his wife, Princess Isabel, in 1884. A national historic monument, it is now used for concerts and exhibitions. Nearby, the **Casa de Santos Dumont** (open: Tues–Sun 9.30am–5pm) commemorates the Brazilian aviation pioneer, a contemporary of the Wright brothers, who made his first flight in October 1906 and is known to Brazilians as the 'Father of Aviation'.

Father of Aviation

A growing number of historians believe that it is Alberto Santos Dumont who should be credited with the first mechanical flight, rather than the Wright brothers. The reasoning is that the Wright brothers' flight of December 1903 was a 'glided flight', their first powered flight only coming in May 1908. Santos Dumont had first flown his plane, the *14-bis*, in October 1906. By November 1906 officials of the Aero-Club du France had seen the *14-bis* cover 220m (722ft) in 21 seconds, the first registered and independently witnessed flight of more than 100m (330ft).

Land of the Coffee Barons

In the 19th century, the cultivation of coffee was at its apogee in the state of Rio de Janeiro. Coffee barons prospered, using slaves to cultivate the crop. With the abolition of slavery in 1888, the inability to replant depleted lands, and the fall of international coffee prices, the coffee industry crashed. But many of the grand plantations, called *fazendas*, remain.

Vale do Paraíba

Stretching to the west of Rio, on the way to the state of Minas Gerais, the **Vale do Paraíba** is infused with reminders of its former grandeur. Today, 18 *fazendas* scattered throughout the mountainous, robustly green valley welcome visitors. Several are even memorable places for overnight stays.

Near **Barra do Piraí** are two *fazendas* that operate as hotels (if you don't wish to stay, you can visit the plantation for

The historic Fazenda Ponte Alta

a small fee). While providing an incomparable window onto the rise and fall of the coffee barons, they also offer a glimpse of a sad past, as many of the rooms are former slaves' quarters.

Hotel Fazenda Arvoredo (tel: 024 2447-2001; <www.hotelarvoredo.com.br>), built in 1858 by the Baron of Santa Maria, is a monumental mansion at the end of a long drive and massive lawn. The large house forms an 'L' shape with the slaves' quarters, called the *senzala*. In the middle of the 18th century, 250 slaves worked to harvest coffee here.

Pousada Fazenda Ponte Alta (tel: 024 2443-5159; <www.pontealta.com.br>) is a beautiful farmhouse behind stables. José Luiz Gomes, who would earn the title of Barão de Mambucaba, constructed the plantation in 1830. Like most plantations, it has a chapel built right into the house.

Fazenda São Joao da Prosperidade, open only for visits (no accommodation), dates to the beginning of the coffee era in the early 19th century. It is more rustic than the elegant estates built in the 1860s and 1870s. Look for the original stove and the small *alcova*, a room without windows where virgin daughters were kept from the roaming eyes of visitors.

Vassouras and Conservatória

The present size of Vassouras and Conservatória belies their importance during the coffee heyday, but the well-preserved architecture in each hints at it. Founded in 1857, **Vassouras** was the capital of the coffee district. The lovely **Praça Barão de Campo Belo** has as its centrepieces a water fountain (1845) and a church, the **Igreja de Nossa Senhora da Conceição** (1853), which offers a commanding view of the valley and its former coffee lands. Behind the church is a road lined by a row of massive fig trees. The cemetery down the street is filled with the mausoleums of coffee barons and their families.

Campo Belo square is ringed by the neoclassical mansions of the families who built their empires here, including the former palace of the Baron of Ribeirão (1860); Casa de Cultura Tancredo Neves, the newly-restored former residence of Francisco José Teixeira de Souza; and City Hall.

Just beyond the plaza are the **Estação Ferroviária**, the old railway station, which looks plucked from the English countryside, and the **Casa de Hera**, where a visit is essential for a glimpse at how the coffee barons lived. The ivy-covered house (the source of its name) is replete with rare porcelain, French furniture, rococo public rooms and heirlooms of the family estate of Joaquim Teixeira Leite.

Near Vassouras are several well-maintained *fazendas*, living museums complete with period antiques. Open to the public (by appointment) is **Fazenda Cachoeira**, the former coffee estate of the Baron of Vassouras, Francisco José Teixeira Leite. Other coffee plantations worth visiting in the area are **Fazenda Secretário** and **Fazenda São Luiz de Boa Sorte**.

It's obvious why this land was originally so well suited for coffee cultivation. Green hills extend as far as one can see. Along the drive west to **Conservatória**, you pass through an 80-m (260-ft) tunnel carved out of a hill by slaves in the 19th century. Exiting it, you emerge into Conservatória, a town with exuberantly-painted colonial houses and a lush central plaza. It's known as 'the music city'; on Friday and Saturday evenings, serenaders take to the streets to court lovers and entertain onlookers. They set out from the **Museu da Seresta** (Serenade Museum) on Rua Osvaldo Fonseca.

BÚZIOS

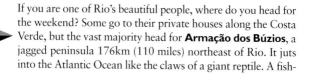

If you are one of Rio's beautiful people, where do you head for the weekend? Some go to their private houses along the Costa Verde, but the vast majority head for **Armação dos Búzios**, a jagged peninsula 176km (110 miles) northeast of Rio. It juts into the Atlantic Ocean like the claws of a giant reptile. A fishing village that won the hearts of the jet set, it's often referred to as the St-Tropez of Brazil. With transparent, Caribbean-blue waters, low white houses, abundant vegetation, 23 beaches of endless variety, excellent fishing, sailing and diving, and an up-and-coming golf course, Búzios is built for fun.

While it remains one of the most beautiful – and expensive – spots in the state of Rio de Janeiro, it is by no means a quiet fishing village any more. This is where the likes of Madonna and U2 come after playing Rio. Búzios continues to expand faster than any other part of the state; restaurants, shopping centres and *pousadas* just keep springing up.

As a visitor to Rio you might want to take advantage of going to Búzios during the week, when it will be even more pleasing and relaxed, and much simpler to get in to the best *pousadas* and restaurants, most based in and around rua das Pedras. The beaches will also be considerably less crowded.

Olho de Boi is one of many lovely beaches at Búzios

WHAT TO DO

FESTIVALS AND FOLKLORE

Carnaval

Rio's legendary annual outburst of music, colour and *alegria* (joy) is probably even more dazzling than you imagined. *Carioca* Carnaval surpasses all other pageants and festivals in the world. Even Hollywood, with the biggest budget in history, couldn't come close to producing such an authentic outpouring of emotion and energy.

Although it's a breathtaking spectacle, at its most basic, Carnaval is an expression of popular culture. More than half a million people – all in costumes they may have paid a large chunk of their annual salary for – march, dance and sing their hearts out in the organised samba school parades. Thousands more revel, in and out of fancy dress, at parties and informal secondary parades. High society and many tourists, including foreigners, join the frenzy in exclusive and fashionable masquerade balls. Whether neighbourhood children with makeshift snare drums or a band of polished musicians perform the music, though, samba during Carnaval is almost ridiculously contagious.

In Rio, the last fling before the austere Lenten season starts in earnest the Friday before Shrove Tuesday (Mardi Gras). It goes on for five days and five nights – more than 100 hours of almost non-stop revelry.

Until the middle of the 19th century, Carnaval in Rio was an aimless and often unseemly outbreak of water fights and practical jokes, derived from Portuguese tradition. In 1855 a band of young men donned colourful costumes and marched to

Ballet on the Feast day of St Sebastian, Rio's patron saint

music. The idea caught fire with the public, other groups were formed, and special marches were composed for the bands. Soon the music evolved into Brazilian forms of light-hearted *choros* and sombre *ranchos*. After World War I, the pace picked up with the invention of the musical form samba, and the groups of revellers became bigger and better disciplined.

The modern era began in 1928 with the organisation of the first *escola de samba* – not a school at all, but a confraternity of Carnaval celebrants united in their dedication to perfecting the music, dancing, costumes and floats. Several more *escolas* soon followed, and by 1933 a formal jury had been established to select the parade's best group. Ever since, competition for Carnaval honours has been every bit as exciting to the *cariocas* as football's World Cup and the locals have become as passionate about supporting their 'school' of choice, as they are about their football teams.

Carnaval parade

Mounting Excitement

Weeks before the holiday, you can feel the excitement begin to sweep the city, as local enthusiasts rehearse for Carnaval in the streets. The *bateria* (band of drummers) pounds out an astounding racket for the director, who cues them with a whistle. The rhythm is as precise as a machine.

On the Friday before Shrove Tuesday, flimsy kiosks suddenly appear on street corners, selling last-minute costume-party ideas. Along Avenida Rio Branco, normally a sober street of banks and offices, the cheerful decorations are up and workmen are busy covering the shop windows with temporary wooden defences. In the evening, the Carnaval king and queen receive the key to the city. Then the first Carnaval club parades past, but this is still minor-league play; the real samba stars won't show themselves for another two days.

On Saturday night, the parades take place in half a dozen locations. At the main site, the Sambódromo, or Passarela do Samba stadium, million-dollar grandstands and VIP viewing booths are filled. But the major *escolas* are still waiting in the wings; they parade in two groups of six, one on Sunday and one on Monday. Packed into the Sambódromo's stands, 60,000 people dance and sing with abandon. The members of each *escola*, divided into 40 disciplined platoons called *alas*, come dressed as Indians, 18th-century lords and ladies, pirates, harlequins, mandarins and animals.

Each samba school chooses a theme *(enredo)* for itself, which it illustrates with music and colour. A float *(carro alegórico)* setting the theme appears first, followed by a small group of dignified gentlemen – the officials of the *escola (comissão de frente)* – who salute the jury and the audience. Other obligatory elements include at least one group of young dancers (sometimes these are small children), as well as a beautiful standard-bearer *(porta-bandeira)* and her fast-dancing es-

Ticket tips

For tickets to the top samba school parades (which for visitors will range from about US $150 to more than $1,000) you should check with travel agents and tour operators in your home country as they are able to reserve space through authorised Brazilian ground agents. Trying to purchase a ticket in Rio on arrival can be considerably more difficult and often more expensive. Even at the last minute, however, your hotel concierge should be able to score you a ticket, but at a price.

cort, both usually wearing 18th-century finery. Young women in elaborate costumes are followed by considerably older ladies, dressed as *Baianas* (women of Bahia). In all, vast armies – as many as 4,000 girls and boys, women and men, in outlandish costumes – march, dance, strut or swivel past the stands.

Somewhere in the first half of the *desfile* (parade) marches the *bateria*, the ensemble of amazingly eloquent percussion instruments. Everyone in the cast, including the roving platoon leaders, gleefully sings the school's own samba in perfect time to the drums.

All the *escolas* are severely judged, on criteria ranging from rhythm and harmony to choreography, timing and overall motion. The official results, which detonate heated joy, despair and controversy all over Rio, are announced the following Thursday. Two days later, all the winners parade again before enthusiastic crowds.

Fancy Dress Balls

In the weeks before Carnaval proper, the Carnaval season moves into top gear. It is, after all, the height of the summer holidays for most Brazilians. Many clubs, organisations and major hotels sponsor Carnaval balls, with tickets normally on sale to the public. At the chic parties, of which the ball held on the Saturday of Carnaval at the Copacabana Palace sets the standard, evening dress or fantasy costumes are specified. Special theme balls, such as the Gay Ball and the Red & Black Ball, in honour of the Flamengo football club, are held at La Scala or Help, and are raucous institutions. Many of these balls aren't for the prudish; you'll see more breasts, *bundas* (posteriors) and simulated acts of sex than you would find on an adult television channel. If you can't go, you can watch the gyrating on TV.

Glamorous and amusing costumes, over-the-top decorations, sweaty rhythms and the lusty enthusiasm (to put it politely) of the participants make Carnaval balls outstanding parties by any standards. Newspapers, magazines and the local tourist authority, Riotur, issue complete lists of the major balls, as well as all the parades. Hotel concierges and porters have private supply lines to hard-to-get tickets and can advise on costume requirements and transport.

Having a ball in fancy dress

Surviving Carnival

Carnaval in Rio isn't violent, but the chance of running into a drunk driver (or vice versa) does increase exponentially every February, so be careful when driving or walking. Thieves are also on the lookout for tourists (both Brazilians and foreigners) whose wits may temporarily escape them, so don't wear ostentatious jewellery or carry more money than is necessary.

The lasciviousness and hedonism of Carnaval can be enticing. While you can dance with anybody at the Carnaval balls, the smiles and flirtatious gestures of Brazilian women are not necessarily invitations. A gruff and/or inebriated boyfriend or husband may be lurking in the shadows. Discretion all round can be a lifesaver. Every year at Carnaval men meet gorgeous women who, once in a hotel room, reveal themselves not to be women at all. Some of Rio's most beautiful women are men, so ask some strategic questions if that's not your interest.

Finally, if you can't take the frantic Carnaval tempo, you're not alone. Thousands of *cariocas* head for the hills or travel abroad every year to avoid the noise and the mobs. The key is, don't go to Rio at Carnaval time if you don't want to take part. You would be better off visiting the city at any other time of the year. And it will be less expensive.

If you can't be in Rio during Carnaval or would rather experience it in a less frenzied forum, some nightclubs in Rio feature talented and attractive samba dancers in Las Vegas-like revues year-round (though the often-cheesy shows are poor approximations of the real thing). Cidade do Samba (Samba City), in downtown Rio, also gives a year-round flavour of Carnaval with an authentic samba show on most Thursday evenings. During the three months preceding Carnaval, it is possible to attend one of the real samba school rehearsals. Check with Riotur or your hotel concierge for details.

Finally, remember that Carnaval is a movable feast. All you need to know is that the main action in Rio takes place from the Friday prior to and up to Ash Wednesday. This can vary from early February to early March, depending on the date of Easter. For dates in the coming years, *see page 113*.

New Year

The New Year celebrations in Rio, known as **Reveillon**, have grown among those in the know to become almost as big an attraction as Carnaval itself. The celebrations, based on and around Copacabana Beach, are one of the most spectacular ways of seeing in the New Year anywhere in the world.

On 31 December, over three million people, the vast majority dressed from head to toe in white, will make their way down to the beach at Copacabana. As well as being New Year's Eve, it is also the feast of Iemanjá, goddess of the sea, and various groups will have built elaborate altars in her honour and will prepare to place their offerings in the sea. Just about every apartment along the beach, and certainly all the hotels, will host parties and the focal point to kick off the celebrations will be a huge fireworks display at midnight that covers the whole of Copacabana. The party will carry on through the night with live music on stages all along the beach. Many hotels start serving special breakfasts from 5am onwards.

New Year fireworks

Other Events

Festas Juninas (June Festivals) is a grouping of celebrations honouring three Catholic saints: John, Anthony and Peter. The parties at the end of the month for John and Peter are especially festive. One of the year's biggest religious celebrations is the **Festa da Penha**, held every Sunday in October at Igreja de Penha in northern Rio. On the year's most solemn holiday, **Sexta-feira da Paixão** (Good Friday), actors dressed in biblical-era costumes proceed through the city retracing the events of the Way of the Cross.

Afro-Brazilian traditions fuel some of the most vivid events in Rio de Janeiro. The two main Afro-Brazilian religions, **Umbanda** and **Candomblé**, both have a strong presence in Rio, and it's possible to attend some of their celebrations and rituals. You will occasionally see flyers advertising these events, but be warned that most announced in this way are no more authentic than the big Las Vegas-style samba shows put on at barbecue houses. To attend a genuine ceremony you may need the help of a local insider. Most of these ceremonies are held in *favelas* and other hard-to-get-to areas.

Capoeira is an Afro-Brazilian form of expression that combines dance and martial arts. Slave owners, who feared the slaves' physi-

Umbanda ritual

cal ability to rebel, outlawed fighting, so the slaves disguised their training as dance. If you don't see *capoeira* in a nightclub, you may bump into it (you don't want it to bump into you) at a market place or in a busy square. While attendants beat drums and pluck a single-stringed instrument called a *berimbau*, the dancer-fighters perform athletic handsprings, spins and flips according to rules as arcane as those of kung fu.

For more information contact Riotur (<www.riodejaneiro-turismo.com.br>), which also issues an annual calendar of events of interest to visitors.

NIGHTLIFE

Rio de Janeiro is proudly nocturnal, with a wide variety of activities, from big, brassy nightclubs and chic discos to friendly jazz bars and informal samba clubs. The local newspapers *O Globo* and *Jornal do Brasil*, and the weekly newsmagazine, *Vejá*, publish listings of what is happening around town. Because of the very nature of the *cariocas*, what is 'hot' one week can be only 'warm' or even 'cold' just a week later. To find out what is 'hot', just ask local people on your arrival. You can also check on Ticketmaster (<www.ticketmaster.com.br>) or Ingresso (<www.ingresso.com.br>).

Live music. Fans of Brazilian music can catch live performances of bossa nova and MPB (Música Popular Brasileira), samba and *pagode*, *chorinho* and *forró*. Showrooms and clubs to look into include Canecão (Botafogo; <www.canecao petrobras.com.br>), Claro Hall (Barra da Tijuca; <www.ticketmaster.com.br>), Vivo Rio (Flamengo; <www.vivorio.com.br>), Circo Voador (Lapa; <www.circovoador.com.br>), Melt (Leblon), Bar do Tom (Leblon), Allegro Bistro (Copacabana), Modern Sound (Copacabana), Carioca da Gema (Lapa), Scenarium (Lapa), Esch Café (Leblon), Vinicius (Ipanema), Ballroom (Botafogo) and Hard Rock Café (Barra da Tijuca).

Concerts. Rio has a vibrant programme of concerts, recitals and operas, often with celebrated foreign artists. Most of the key venues are in the centre of town and include Rio's plush Teatro Municipal (<www.theatromunicipal.rj.gov.br>) and the Sala Cecília Meireles (<www.salaceciliameireles.com.br>).

Samba shows. A number of tourist-oriented shows hint at Carnaval – at least in terms of the costumes and fancy footwork. The best known is Plataforma (<www.plataforma 1.com.br>), a Vegas wannabe for large groups. For something more authentic, visit the actual samba schools or Cidade do Samba (<http://cidadedosambarj.globo.com>).

Dancing. For an unusual but authentically *carioca* night out, try a *gafieira* (dance hall), where locals go to shake up the dance floor. The classic dance halls are Estudantina and Elite. Another, more sophisticated hall is the 100-year-old Asa Branca in Lapa. Less Brazilian are the discos. Baronneti (Ipanema),

Showgirls

Bombar (Leblon), Bukowski (Botafogo), Fosfobox (Copacabana), Bunker (Copacabana), Nova Lounge (Ipanema), 00 (Gávea), This Week (Centro) and Melt (Leblon) are recent hot spots with the locals, while for the gay community the top picks are Le Boy and La Girl (Copacabana) and Dama de Ferro (Ipanema). Help (Copacabana) is huge and a bit predatory.

Bars and botequims. This is where you'll see *cariocas* at their finest (the night-time equivalent of the beaches). Expect

Music of Rio

Rio is one of the world's most musical cities, and not just at Carnaval time. It is home to both samba and bossa nova and also to countless Brazilian musicians and composers who cover every Brazilian musical form from MPB (Música Popular Brasileira) to frevo, from *choro to forró*.

You are never going to be far from music in Rio as the local Cariocas tend to tap out a tune on a simple matchbox or table top, even as they sip a cold beer. Going to a show with the locals is a special treat, it does not matter if it is the intimate setting of one of the jazz bars, or in the larger concert venues of Canecão, Vivo Rio or the Claro Hall. Even the big outdoor festivals, such as Rock in Rio, are special.

Brazil has a vast spectrum of musical talent, but some of the big names to look out for, and in the record shops as well, if you want to pick up a souvenir of time spent in Rio, are Adriana Calcanhoto, Ana Carolina, Babel Gilberto, Caetano Veloso, Carlinhos Brown, Chico Buarque, Daniela Mercury, Gilberto Gil, Ivete Sangalo, João Gilberto, Jorge Benjor, Maria Bethania, Maria Rita, Marisa Monte, Milton Nascimento, Ney Matogrosso, Paralamas do Sucesso, Titãs, Vanessa da Mata and Zeca Pagodinho, to name just a few.

Brazil, of course, has had many great composers and performers who are no longer with us. Among those who continue to shine from beyond the grave are Antonio Carlos Jobim and Elis Regina and, from the world of classical music, Heitor Villa-Lobos.

Dancing the night away

to see spontaneous samba erupt. Lapa is a bohemian area with a lot of energy at weekends; try Asa Branca *(see previous page)*, which is sure to be hopping. Classic *carioca botequims* can be found both in the centre and Zona Sul. Some to note include Bar Luiz (Centro), Boteco Casual (Centro), Bofetada (Ipanema), Bar Lagoa (Lagoa), Bracarense (Leblon) and Jobi (Leblon). Lovers of *cachaça* (sugar-cane alcohol), or the curious, should check out the Academia da Cachaça (Leblon/Barra da Tijuca; <www.academiadacachaca.com.br>), which has *pinga* from all over Brazil.

Erotica. Rio's red light district is not what it used to be, but the erotic clubs that survive are still concentrated in Copacabana and Leme. In most, the drinks are expensive.

SPORTS

Spectator Sports

Futebol. Football is a national passion – some would say religion – and Brazilians are among the world's best, and most creative, players of the game. The national team have won the World Cup on five occasions and Brazil is now preparing to host the tournament in 2014. Rio's favourite teams are Flamengo, Vasco, Botafogo and Fluminense. If you're a fan, seeing a match at Maracanã, the world's biggest football stadium, which once had a capacity of 200,000, will be unforgettable. The main game of the week is usually played on Sunday, kicking off around 5pm or 6pm. Tickets are normally easy to come by or you can opt for an organised tour. A schedule of matches and other sporting events can be found on the site of *O Globo* (<http://oglobo.globo.com/online/esportes/default.asp>).

Horse races. You can check out the horse races at the beautiful Hipódromo do Jockey Club Brasileiro (tel: 2512-9988; <www.jcb.com.br>), in Gávea on Praça Santos Dumont, 31. Races are held on Monday 6.30–10.45pm; Friday 4.30–9pm; and Saturday and Sunday 2–7pm. It is not difficult for foreign visitors to get into the comfortable members' enclosure. The Jockey Club's biggest sporting and social event of the year is the Grande Prêmio Brasil held in August.

Motor races. Because of Rio's proximity to São Paulo, host of the Brazilian Formula One Grand Prix, many fans choose to stay in Rio and fly down for the race, flight time being just 40 minutes.

Crowds at the Maracanã Stadium

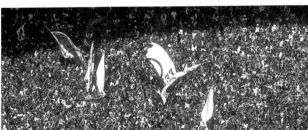

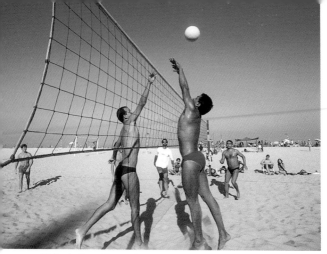

Volleyball on Copacabana

Other sports. The beach is a key venue for sporting activities and during the summer months there are likely to be volleyball, football and even tennis tournaments to watch on Copacabana Beach. Golf can be seen at Itanhangá Golf Club (Barra da Tijuca), which is also the place for polo, and at Gávea Golf Club. Volleyball proper, and basketball, are to be found at Maracanazinho and in other clubs around Rio. In 2007, Rio hosted the Pan American Games.

Participatory Sports

Diving. The best diving in the state of Rio is along the Costa Verde or off Búzios. Those already qualified to dive can join a dive group to go out to the islands off Rio from the Marina da Glória every Saturday and Sunday at 8am (tel: 2266-4041; <www.diversquest.com.br>).

Fishing. Shops all over town sell fishing tackle. You'll find fishermen working the cliffs along Avenida Niemeyer or casting from the side of Sugar Loaf. Deep-sea fishing, for tuna, marlin and dorado, is best near the continental shelf, about 64km (40 miles) from Rio. The best time of year is October to December. Boats from 4–13m (14–42ft) can be chartered from various owners based at the Marina da Glória (tel: 2205-6716; <www.marinadagloria.com.br>).

Golf. Opportunities for golf are rather limited as the clubs in Rio are private. During the week the better hotels can arrange to book a tee-off time at either the Gávea (São Conrado) or Itanhangá (Barra da Tijuca) golf clubs, both of which are world class. There is also a public, six-hole, par-3 course at Golden Green in Barra. Otherwise the best options are the courses outside the city of Rio (<www.fgerj.com.br>) in Búzios, Angra, Teresópolis and Petrópolis.

Hiking. Excellent trails can be found in the Tijuca National Forest, around Sugar Loaf and in the Serra dos Orgãos National Park close to Teresópolis.

Sailing. Boats can be chartered from various owners and companies based at the Marina da Glória (*see above*).

Surfing. The best beaches are Arpoador, Barra and Grumari.

Tennis. The Sheraton, Inter-Continental and Copacabana Palace hotels all have their own courts. Most of the other courts are to be found in private clubs.

Other sports. It is possible to play just about any sport in Rio; it is just a question of asking. The respective foreign communities play sports like baseball, bowls, darts and even rugby.

Unique Sightseeing Opportunities

Bay cruises. For schooner cruises of Guanabara Bay and down the coast to Angra dos Reis, try Saveiros Tours (tel: 2225-6064; <www.saveiros.com.br>) or the Marina da Glória (*see above*).

Favela visits. To organise a visit to a *favela* (do not attempt to go on your own), contact Marcelo Armstrong of Favela Tours (tel: 3322-2727; <www.favelatour.com.br>).

Hang-gliding. Tandem hang- and para-gliders (no experience necessary) take off from Pedra Bonita above São Conrado and soar over Praia do Pepino to land on the beach. Several operators provide instructors and even a camera to shoot pictures of you in the sky. Contact the Associação de Vôo Livre (tel: 3322-0266; <www.abvl.com.br>) for a list of operators.

Helicopter rides. Flights over Rio offer spectacular vantage points. Starting from less than US$50, they leave from Morro da Urca, Dona Marta and the Lagoa. Contact Helisight (tel: 2511-2141; <www.helisight.com.br>).

SHOPPING

Gemstones and jewellery. Brazil is one of the major gem-producing countries in the world, and many people come to Brazil to buy indigenous precious stones – said to be as much as 25

Hang-gliding to the beach

percent cheaper than in the US and Europe. They're sold in hotel boutiques, in city-centre shops and on street corners by contrabandists with pockets full of emeralds (or wannabe-emeralds).

A market jewellery stallholder

The most popular buys are amethysts, aquamarines, opals, topaz and tourmalines. But diamonds, emeralds, rubies and sapphires are also mined in Brazil. Check with your consulate concerning customs regulations if you are considering a purchase. The two best-known and most reputable dealers of gemstones, H. Stern and Amsterdam Sauer, have branches everywhere, including most of the major hotels, and offer free museum/workshop tours. H. Stern's headquarters is in Ipanema, at Rua Visconde de Pirajá, 490 (tel: 2106-0000; <www.hstern.net>); Amsterdam Sauer's is at Avenida Garcia D'Ávila, 105 (tel: 2512-1132; <www.amsterdamsauer.com>).

Gift ideas. Some of the items you may wish to take home from Rio include: art – particularly naïve and primitive works; antiques, from the shops along Rua do Lavradio or the antiques fair; *figas*, the Afro-Brazilian good-luck symbol in the form of a fist (to bring good luck, it must be given as a gift); hand-made hammocks; jacaranda-wood salad bowls and trays; cloth kites, in fighting-bird shapes and bright colours; leather bags, belts, wallets and shoes; musical instruments, such as the *berimbau*; recordings of samba, bossa nova and MPB; and swimsuits (if they're not too risqué for the beaches you frequent). Brazil is also a leader in world fashion and currently many of even the most fashionable boutiques offer excellent value when compared with Europe and North America.

Ipanema boutique

Where to Shop

The most sophisticated boutiques are in Ipanema. Copacabana has more variety, except for clothing, and prices are generally lower. *Cariocas*, however, head to the shopping centres, which have branches of most of the top boutiques. They include Rio Sul Shopping (Botafogo), which is closest to the hotels in Copacabana, Shopping Leblon, closest to Ipanema and Leblon, and Ipanema, BarraShopping (Barra da Tijuca) and the São Conrado Fashion Mall (São Conrado).

Fairs and markets. All over Rio street markets selling brilliantly-coloured fruits, vegetables and flowers provide a lively free show, usually once a week in each neighbourhood. One of the best takes place on Friday morning in Praça de Paz in Ipanema. At weekends, several fairs or markets of more specific tourist interest are scheduled. Feirarte, or the Hippie Fair, is a busy arts and crafts fair held at Praça General Osório in Ipanema every Sunday 9am–6pm; it's a good place for paintings, leatherwork, carvings, tapestries, jewellery and other gifts. The Feira do Nordeste is probably the most exotic and memorable of all the markets, but is not aimed at tourists. Every Sunday from 6am until 1pm you can mingle with dancers and musicians, faith healers, patent-medicine demonstrators, and sellers of tropical fish, holy pictures, spices and clothing. You can also sample authentic food from northeastern Brazil. It's at Campo de São Cristóvão in the northern zone of Rio; take any bus marked São Cristóvão or grab a cab. Feirarte II, Thursday and

Friday 8am–6pm at the Praça XV de Novembro, offers dolls, jewellery, embroidery, leather goods and musical instruments (and Bahian food). At the Feira de Antiquários, Saturday 8am–5pm at Praça Marechal Âncora (near Praça XV de Novembro) you may spot old Portuguese tiles, porcelain or silver.

CHILDREN

Flamengo Park. On Sunday traffic is barred from the highway through the park, permitting roller skaters, cyclists and joggers to fan out over the asphalt. One way to see the park is to take the *trenzinho* (little train), a tractor-drawn sightseeing vehicle that covers most of the grounds in 25 minutes. Children enjoy it most, but adults are fully welcome aboard.

Jardim Zoológico. Like many of the visitors, the 2,000 animals at Rio's zoo (Quinta da Boavista; tel: 3878-4200; open: Tues–Sun 9am–4.30pm; <www.rio.rj.gov.br/riozoo>) seem seized by tropical languor except at the official feeding times. Along with the usual run of lions, camels, elephants and monkeys, the zoo has some 1,600 birds, and a variety of panthers.

Lagoa Pedalos. Pedalos can be rented on the calm waters of the Lagoa (Parque do Cantagalo), daily 8am–6pm.

Theme Parks

Rio de Janeiro has a number of theme parks, the majority and largest of which are based in Barra da Tijuca. Terra Encantada (Avenida Ayrton Senna, 2800; tel: 2421-9444; open: Thur–Sat 2–9pm, Sun noon–9pm) is not quite up to the standards of Disney but is a good place to take the kids if they grow restless sightseeing or tired of the beach. Close by is the city's main water park, Rio Water Planet (Estrada das Bandeirantes, 24000; tel: 2428-9000; open: Sat–Sun 10am–5pm). Two of Rio's main shopping centres, BarraShopping and Rio Sul, also have play and amusement areas.

Calendar of Events

1 January New Year's Day and Festa da Iemanjá (Reveillon): Rio's homage to Iemanjá, the goddess of the sea; takes place on and around Copacabana beach.

20 January Dia do São Sebastião: A celebration of St Sebastian, the patron saint of Rio de Janeiro (holiday in Rio de Janeiro).

February/March Carnaval: movable feast that starts on the Friday before Shrove Tuesday and comes to a close on Ash Wednesday.

1 March Dia da Fundação da Cidade: Celebration of the city's founding in 1565 by Estácio de Sá.

March/April Sexta-feira da Paixão: Good Friday.

21 April Tiradentes: National holiday.

1 May Labour Day: National holiday.

June Festas Juninas (June Festivals): Celebration of saints Anthony, Peter and John. Rio marathon.

3 July Festa do São Pedro do Mar: Festival honouring St Peter, the patron saint of fishermen.

August Grande Premio do Brasil: Brazil's most important horserace, held at the Hipódromo do Jockey Club Brasileiro.

15 August Festa de Nossa Senhora da Glória do Outeiro: Feast of the Assumption in Glória.

September–October Rio Film Festival.

7 September Dia de Independência do Brasil: Independence Day.

October Festa da Penha: Lively religious festival at Igreja Nossa Senhora da Penha. Brazilian Formula One Grand Prix (São Paulo).

12 October Nossa Senhora Aparaceida: National holiday celebrating the patron saint of Brazil.

2 November All Souls' Day.

15 November Republic Day: National holiday celebrating the proclamation of the Republic.

15 December Summer holidays start.

31 December Celebração de Fim do Ano and Festa de Iemanjá: New Year's Eve and Reveillon.

EATING OUT

In the melting pot of Brazil, three different concepts of a square meal have melded deliciously. The Indians contributed vegetables, grains and an appreciation of seafood; the Portuguese, their stews and their sweet tooth; and the African slaves added new spices and sauces.

Rio was long São Paulo's poorer cousin in terms of dining options, but since the 1980s its array of international cuisines – French, German, Spanish, Portuguese and Italian, as well as food from more exotic locales – has improved significantly. The sushi fad has exploded here. The most authentic *cariocas* eating experiences, however, are based on four items: meat, served in *churrascarias* (barbecue houses), often *rodízio* style (all you can eat); *feijoada*, the national dish; fish and seafood; and tropical fruits and vegetables. Other indispensable parts of the *cariocas* diet are spicy foods imported from northeastern Brazil, notably Bahia.

The tourist zone, Zona Sul, contains the majority of the city's best restaurants. Also worth exploring, at lunchtime, is the central business district, which has a distinguished range of res-

Feijoada, the national dish

Buffet in a *churrascaria* restaurant

taurants. Some of Rio's finest and most elegant dining is to be found in the restaurants of the top hotels in Copacabana and Ipanema, most notably the Copacabana Palace (Cipriani), Fasano (Fasano El Mare) and Sofitel Rio (Le Pré Catelan). You won't find just tourists and businessmen on expense account, as *cariocas* who can afford it frequently dine at hotels on special occasions. One craze is for restaurants at which you pay by weight. Called 'A Kilo' (or 'A Quilo'), they range from *churrascarias* to Lebanese restaurants; many offer a bit of everything. At between R$15 and R$25 per kilo of food, they represent tremendous value, and in many the quality is considerably higher than your average cafeteria. Considered among the best are Celeiro (Leblon), Da Silva (Ipanema), Ekko's Café (Botafogo), Fazendola (Jardim Botânico) and Felini (Leblon). *Botequims (see page 83)* are good places for simple meals. Vegetarians will find a number of 'natural food' and salad-oriented options.

Brazilian Cuisine

The national dish, *feijoada*, is a stew that contains 18 or 19 ingredients and takes hours to prepare. It may take longer to digest, which is why you'd be wise not to order it at night. Typically, *feijoada* is served on Wednesday and Saturday, but most *cariocas* eat it at lunch on Saturday. It's a feast of black beans with smoked sausage, pork products (tongue, tail, ear, etc.) and dried beef, flavoured with onions, garlic, chives, tomatoes, parsley and hot peppers, then served with boiled rice, shredded kale, fried manioc flour, and – a brilliant afterthought – fresh slices of orange. It's almost obligatory to start or accompany this meal with a *batida* or *caipirinha* aperitif *(see page 97).*

A Taste of the Northeast

In the cuisine of northeastern Brazil, Indian, African and European currents meet. Rio has several good restaurants specialising in these spicy delights, which include:

Acarajé. A large fritter made from a batter of ground beans, deep-fried in boiling *dendê* oil, the yellowish palm oil indispensable to Bahian cooking. The resulting dumpling is split down the middle and liberally filled with *vatapá* (see below), dried shrimp and hot *malagueta* pepper sauce. It is served as a starter or snack. Be careful; it can be wickedly hot.

Vatapá. This calls to mind shrimp creole, but it's more complicated, with subtly interacting flavours. The ingredients may include shrimp, fish, grated coconut, ground peanuts, cashew nuts, tomatoes, onions, hot peppers, ginger, coriander, olive oil, *dendê* oil, pepper and salt. This is thickened with bread crumbs and served with rice cooked in coconut milk.

Xinxim. (pronounced 'shing-shing'). What differentiates this Bahian chicken stew from all other chicken-in-the-pot recipes is the addition of ground, dried shrimp and the use of hot spices and *dendê* oil. Approach the hot sauce served on the side with caution!

Seafood selection

From Brazil's southernmost state of Rio Grande do Sul comes *churrasco*, which is Gaucho-style barbecued meat. *Cariocas* and tourists alike enjoy dining at *churrascarias*, where strips of beef, plus sausages, chicken or chops are skewered and roasted over charcoal. Cuts to look for include *picanha* (rump steak), *fraldinha* (bottom sirloin) and *ponta de agulha* (short ribs). At all-you-can-eat *rodízios* the waiters arrive with one skewer after another, tempting you first with a sausage, then a chop, then a steak, and so on, until you've had enough. You don't have to know the language, but you certainly need a big appetite. Rio's most famous *rodízios* include Porcão (Botafogo/Ipanema/Barra da Tijuca), Marius (Leme) and Espaço Brasa Leblon (Leblon).

Many Rio restaurants deal primarily in fish and seafood. Look for *zarzuela de mariscos*, a thick Spanish version of a bouillabaisse, or the Portuguese variants, *caldeirada* or *frutos do mar ensopados*. *Moquequas* (of fish, shrimp or crab) are a style of Bahian fish stew prepared in a covered clay pot. When they eat fish, *cariocas* generally prefer a thick fillet, so in many restaurants you'll find dishes described vaguely as *filet de peixe* (fish fillet). The fish in question often turns out to be *badejo* (bass), tasty in spite of its anonymity, but sometimes overwhelmed by a thick tomato sauce. You can also get excellent *linguado* (sole). The sauce called *belle meunière* is a butter sauce complicated or complimented, depending on your point of view, by the addition of shrimp, mushrooms, asparagus, capers and whatever else will make it seem luxurious. In Portuguese restaurants, you can choose from many varieties of *bacalhau*, dried salt cod, usually baked in a rich sauce.

Hurry-up Food

In every part of Rio de Janeiro, you'll find lunch-counter restaurants advertising *galetos*, spring chickens barbecued over charcoal. They make fast, cheap and often delicious meals. Stand-up snack bars, known as *lanchonetes*, are everywhere. They serve *lanches* – meaning snacks, not lunches, which is what you might guess. These are the places to try Brazilian appetisers, such as codfish balls, Lebanese *kibe*, shrimp pies or *pão de queijo* (cheese bread). Home-made Bahian treats like *acarajé* and *vatapá* are sold on the streets.

Drinks

Brazil's most popular cocktail, the *caipirinha*, is akin to a Mexican *margarita*, but instead of tequila, the firewater is *cachaça*, distilled from sugar cane. Ice and lemon (or a sweeter cousin, *limão de Persia*) soften the blow of this potent concoction. After just a few, you'll recognise that it tastes of Brazil. A *batida* is a cocktail – usually whipped up in a blender – of *cachaça*, ice, sugar and fruit juice.

Caipirinhas, the national drink

Given the generally tropical temperatures, Brazilians don't drink a lot of wine, but that should not stop you from enjoying the excellent local wines, plus those from neigbouring Chile and Argentina. *Cariocas* in general stick to Brazilian beer, a great national asset – always served very cold. Draught beer – *chopp* – is the favourite, but some restaurants only serve bottled beer, usually in large bottles. Look for harder-to-find bottled beers such as Bohemia and Cerpa. If you can't get them, an Antârtica or Brahma *bem geladinha* (well chilled) will do just fine.

Coffee, usually espresso-like *cafezinho*, is strong. Brazilians like their coffee very sweet, and very often.

Juices and Other Thirst-Quenchers

In the tropical heat, you'll work up a healthy thirst. But no matter where you find yourself, relief is close at hand. On the beach, barefoot salesmen shuffle past you every other minute offering soft drinks, mineral water, beer or paper cups filled with iced lemonade or *mate* (pronounced *mah-chee*) from their over-the-shoulder tanks. Here the *mate* is served very cold and sweetened; it tastes like tea with overtones of tobacco. Another typically Brazilian drink, bottled and swaggering with caffeine, is *guaraná*; it's made from a fruit from the Amazon forest and tastes a bit like cream soda. A great thirst-quencher in the tropical heat is *agua de coco*, coconut water (it's a natural rehydrant).

Above all, though, look for the bars overflowing with fresh fruit. They serve *sucos* (juices), sometimes as many as 30 or 40 different fruits, some of them exotic fruits you've never seen or heard of, squeezed as you watch. Don't limit yourself to the delicious orange juice; try some tropical specialities like *cajú* (cashew-apple), *mamão* (papaya), *maracujá* (passion fruit), *manga* (mango) and others. More exotic still are fruits from the north and northeast, including *graviola*, *cupuaçú*, *tamarindo* and the fashionable fruit of the moment, *açai*, dark purple and with a distinctive, strong taste. You can also find wonderful sorbets made from these fruits (one of the best ice cream parlours is called Mil Frutas).

To Help You Order…

Could we have a table? **Queríamos uma mesa.**

I'd like a/an/some… **Queria…**

beer	**uma cerveja**	milk	**leite**
bill (the)	**a conta**	mineral water	**água mineral**
bread	**pão**	napkin	**guardanapo**
butter	**manteiga**	potatoes	**batatas**
coffee	**café (cafezinho)**	rice	**arroz**
dessert	**sobremesa**	salad	**salada**
fish	**peixe**	sandwich	**sanduíche**
fruit	**fruta**	soup	**sopa**
ice cream	**sorvete**	sugar	**açúcar**
meat	**carne**	tea	**chá**
menu (the)	**o cardápio**	wine	**vinho**

…and Read the Menu

abacaxi	pineapple	**framboesas**	raspberries
alho	garlic	**frango**	chicken
almôndegas	meatballs	**frito**	fried
arroz	rice	**goiaba**	guava
assado	roasted	**grelhado**	grilled
azeitonas	olives	**lagosta**	spiny lobster
bacalhau	cod	**laranja**	orange
badejo	sea bass	**legumes**	vegetables
bife	beefsteak	**limão**	lemon
bolo	cake	**melancia**	watermelon
cabrito	kid	**morangos**	strawberries
camarão	shrimp	**ovo**	egg
caranguejo	crab	**peixe**	fish
carneiro	lamb	**pescadinha**	whiting
chouriço	a spicy sausage	**pimentão**	green pepper
costeletas	pork ribs	**queijo**	cheese
feijão	beans	**sobremesa**	dessert
flan	caramel custard	**sorvete**	ice cream

HANDY TRAVEL TIPS

An A–Z Summary of Practical Information

A

ACCOMMODATION

(see also the list of RECOMMENDED HOTELS on page 126)

Most of the year, Rio's hotels meet demand, but during Carnaval up to 400,000 tourists descend on the city without confirmed hotel reservations. If you don't book ahead (for many of the key hotels this means six months in advance) you may find yourself renting an expensive apartment from an agency specialising in holiday rentals or checking in at a motel on the outskirts of town. The same is true for Christmas and New Year. Also note that during Carnaval most of the hotels in Rio are only interested in selling fixed packages that cover the carnival period, so don't plan or expect to come for a one-night stand.

At any time of year, and regardless of how independent you are, it is wise to book a hotel room in advance for at least your first night.

Breakfast isn't necessarily included in the price of a room. In small, inexpensive hotels, a distinction is made between *quarto*, a room with a toilet and basin, and *apartamento*, a room with a separate bathroom.

I'd like a single/double room	**Eu gostaria de um quarto de solteiro/de casal**
with toilet	**com banheiro**
with bath/shower.	**com banheiro/chuveiro.**
What's the daily rate?	**Quanto é a diária?**

AIRPORTS

Rio's international airport is Aeroporto do Antonio Carlos Jobim (formerly Aeroporto do Galeão), on Ilha do Governado (tel: 3398-5050). The airport has two terminals that are linked by a moving walkway. The newer, Terminal 2, is home to Varig, Tam and many of the Star Alliance partners such as United and Lufthansa. Most other international airlines use Terminal 1. Just beyond the customs hall, and this is true for both terminals, are information desks operated by Riotur, Rio's official tourist agency, where multilingual receptionists answer questions, distribute pamphlets, and help with hotel reservations. The airport has banks for changing money and a selection of ATM machines. On leaving Brazil there is no bank beyond passport control (flight side) to change reais back into other currencies. The duty-free stores now finally accept reais but it's still best to spend or get rid of your reais at the shops before going through passport control.

Immediately outside the customs hall are the desks of the authorised taxi companies that charge standard fares from the airport according to destination; you pay on the spot in advance and give the receipt to the driver. You can also pre-pay for your return taxi ride to the airport, something worth considering given the generous discounts offered. The trip to the business centre takes 30 to 40 minutes, to the beach zone, up to an hour if you arrive during the morning rush hour. Taxis are not expensive and are the best and safest way to get to your accommodation. A cheaper way to reach central Rio and the beach hotels is by bus. A convenient, air-conditioned bus, called a *frescão*, travels from the international airport to Santos Dumont airport and then along the beaches. The returning bus passes along the beaches, but stops are not well indicated, and the bus passes infrequently. In 2007 a shuttle van service between the airport and many of the main hotels was introduced (tel: 7842-2490; <www.shuttlerio.com.br>). An airport tax is levied on departure – this may or may not have been included in your ticket. Payment can be made either in dollars or reais.

The best shops for gifts are on the third floor of Terminal 1. All the best stores, including those for buying reading material for the flight, are to be found before going through passport control.

Santos Dumont Airport, Rio's second airport, is close to the centre. Most flights are between Rio and São Paulo with other domestic services operating from the international airport. To get there from the Zona Sul resorts, take any air-conditioned bus going to the centre of Rio – they'll let you off within easy walking distance of the airport.

B

BUDGETING FOR YOUR TRIP

All Latin American economies tend to be volatile, so what is true today may not necessarily be so when you get to Brazil. For example, Rio was a cheap getaway during much of the 1980s, but became one of the world's most expensive cities in the early 1990s. Since currency reform in 1994, prices have tended to be relatively stable, and Brazil once again offers excellent value to North American and European visitors. The unit of currency is the real (R$; plural, reais).

Transport costs. Flights to Brazil are fairly expensive, especially in high season. Transport on the ground is quite reasonable; local and intra-state buses are very cheap, and taxis are an affordable option for getting around the city. Remember when travelling within Brazil that the country is larger than the USA. The choice can often be 48 hours on a bus or six hours on a plane. If you are going to be travelling in Brazil, look at getting an airpass prior to your arrival. Brazil also has some low-cost airlines, most notably Gol (<www.voegol.com.br>).

Accommodation. In general, hotels are reasonably priced. Some, but not all, include breakfast in the price of the room.

Meals. The cost of dining in Rio, when compared to major cities in Europe and the US, is very reasonable. Many restaurants have attractively priced *pratos do dia* menus at lunchtime, and some *churrascarias* (barbecue restaurants) offer daytime discounts.

C

CAR HIRE (RENTAL)

Hiring a car in Rio is not cheap. If you're staying in the city, there's no reason to hire a car; do so only for excursions. International and local car-hire agencies have offices at the airports, in the business centre, and in Copacabana, Ipanema, Leblon and other tourist areas. Drivers must be 21 and have held a valid licence for at least two years; you'll also need a credit card and, often, your passport. Third-party insurance is required and usually included in the charge, but make sure the price you are quoted reflects this condition. Collision insurance is a sizable extra. The fine print on contracts always hides clauses that can be troublesome in case of an accident. Read the contract carefully.

You can hire a car from a major company (Interlocadora, Localiza, LocarAlpha, Nobre, Unidas) at the international airport or in the Zona Sul; likewise Hertz, Avis and Budget are based in Copacabana as well as at the airport. Charges start from US$40 a day.

I'd like to hire (rent) a car today/tomorrow for one day/a week.	**Queria alugar um carro para hoje/amanhã por um dia/uma semana.**
Please include full insurance.	**Que inclua um seguro contra todos os riscos, por favor.**
Does that include mileage?	**Isso inclui a quilometragem?**

CLIMATE

Notwithstanding the allure of Carnaval, the best times to travel to Rio to avoid the crowds are April to October. The weather is cooler but never cold, the beaches are still populated, and the summer haze clears. Visitors from the northern hemisphere who come in January usually resist the idea of using a beach umbrella at that time of year, but the afternoon sun during Rio's summer is extremely intense. Make sure you apply sun block generously. In any season, be sure to drink plenty of liquids. Rio's abundant natural juice bars are perfect for pit stops. Above all, take it easy on the beach if you arrive in scorching summer, when it's not unusual to have a string of 32°C (90°F) days with 90 percent humidity.

The driest months of the year are May to October, a time when the temperature is lower and you may actually see some jumpers. The following chart will help you predict Rio's weather:

	J	F	M	A	M	J	J	A	S	O	N	D
°C	26	26	25	24	22	21	21	21	22	22	23	24
°F	85	85	80	75	72	70	70	70	72	72	74	75

CLOTHING

Brazil's relaxed informality may surprise travellers coming from conservative countries. In Rio you'll see tiny tops and short shorts on bank tellers. Shirtless patrons are occasionally barred from some restaurants, however, and a certain degree of modesty is expected when visiting historic churches.

If you visit Rio during its summer, you may need an umbrella, or at the least a cap or hat. Locals rarely wear raincoats because they're too hot. For Rio's winter, pack a light jumper.

Can I try it on?	**Posso experimentar?**
Do you have anything larger/smaller?	**Tem maior/menor?**
I'm just looking.	**So estou olhando.**
Can I pay in dollars?	**Posso pagar em dólares?**
Do you accept credit cards?	**Aceita cartões de crédito?**

CRIME AND SAFETY

The horror stories that have been published in the past that make Rio sound like a tropical Wild West are a bit exaggerated. Petty crime, as in all the world's major cities where tourists congregate, remains a problem, and it's best to take the necessary precautions. Store your valuables in the hotel safe. Take nothing of value to the beach, where sneaky thieves take advantage of careless or unwary tourists. An old trick is for a kid to approach you from one side and ask you the time; he'll pretend not to understand, while behind you one of his partners is picking you clean. More subtly, someone might ask you to guard his shirt while he goes swimming; he tosses the shirt casually over your belongings, and on his return scoops up the lot. Beware of pick-pockets in crowds; keep wallets and bags in front of you. Stay clear of lonely beaches and unlit streets. Avoid displays of jewellery.

Keep in mind that Rio is a busy, cosmopolitan city and not a sleepy tropical resort, and you won't go too far wrong.

Note that possession of even small quantities of drugs can bring up to two years' imprisonment; the authorities make little distinction between marijuana, pills or hard drugs.

Keep safe in the water by remembering that appearances are often deceptive – an apparently mild beach may have a strong undertow. So if the lifeguard hoists a red flag, stay out of the water, no matter how inviting it looks. Never allow children to swim unattended.

I want to report a theft.	**Quero denunciar um roubo.**
I've been robbed.	**Fui roubado.**
Where is the police station?	**Onde é a delegacia da policia?**

CUSTOMS AND ENTRY REQUIREMENTS

Citizens of Australia, Canada, New Zealand and the US require a visa to enter Brazil; even if your airline lets you board, you'll be sent back if you don't have one. Citizens of the UK and most European countries at the time of writing need only a valid passport to enter Brazil, but this is likely to change. Check with your local Brazilian consulate or at <www.brazil.org.uk>.

No vaccinations are required for Rio unless you are arriving from, or have recently visited, countries infected with certain serious dis-eases (cholera, yellow fever, etc.); again the latest regulations can be found at your local Brazilian consulate or <www.brazil.org.uk>. International passengers may purchase duty-free goods for a total of US$500 or the equivalent in another currency on arrival in Brazil, including a restricted amount of alcoholic beverages.

A non-resident may import an unlimited amount of foreign currency and travellers' cheques and a reasonable amount of Brazilian reais, but must declare any amount above R$10,000.

D

DRIVING

The obvious question is: why? Local drivers are not noted for their courtesy, nor are they terribly interested in obeying signals and laws. Even bus drivers sometimes run red lights, especially late at night. Cars may pass you on either side. Pedestrians need to be extremely cautious: they have the lowest priority of all moving objects in Rio.

Rules and regulations. The speed limit is 80km/h (50mph) on all highways, including expressways, 60km/h (37mph) in towns.

Fuel costs. Petrol (gasoline), is more expensive than in the US and comparable to or lower than prices in Europe. Service stations are usually open at night and on Sunday. Make sure that the attendant sets the fuel meter back to zero before filling your tank, and that he uses the correct fuel. Many cars in Brazil run on alcohol-based fuel.

Fill the tank with petrol(gas)/ alcohol, please.	**Encha o tanque de gasolina/ alcool, por favor.**
Check the oil/ tires/battery.	**Poderia verificar o óleo/ os pneus/a bateria?**
I need a can of oil.	**Preciso de uma lata de óleo, por favor.**

Parking *(estacionamento)*. Finding a space is very difficult, especially in the beach areas. Illegal triple parking in the street is quite common. Rio has no parking meters, but some areas have parking wardens *(guardadores autônomos)* who collect a posted fee for two hours' parking. Elsewhere, neighbourhood children or old men often supervise parking, expecting a fee for watching over the car. Hotel parking, in guarded areas, can be comparatively expensive.

If you need help *(ajuda)*. In an emergency, dial the police: 190; ambulance: 193.

I've had a breakdown.	**O meu carro precisa de consertos.**
There's been an accident.	**Houve um acidente.**

Road signs. The streets of Rio are very well identified, with illuminated blue-and-white signs on the street corners. Here is a list of typical road signs that you will encounter:

Cruzamento	Crossroads
Curva perigosa	Dangerous curve
Descida íngreme	Steep hill
Desvio	Detour
Devagar	Slow
Estacionamento proibido	No parking
Mão dupla	Two-way traffic
Mantenha sua direita/esquerda	Keep right/left
Pare	Stop
Pedestres	Pedestrians
Perigo	Danger
Proibida a entrada	No entry
Retorno proibido	No U turn

E

ELECTRICITY

In most places in Rio the current is 110-volts, 60 cycles (the same as in the US). However, some hotels have 220-volt outlets; they are usually marked.

I need an adapter/ a battery, please.	Preciso de um adaptador/ uma pilha, por favor.

EMBASSIES, CONSULATES, HIGH COMMISSIONS

More than 50 consulates and commercial missions operate in the former capital. All embassies are now based in Brasília.

Australia (Honorary Consul): Avenida Presidente Wilson, 231/23, Centro; tel: 3824-4624.

Canada: Avenida Atlântica, 1130, 5th floor, Atlântica Business Center, Copacabana, tel: 2543-3004.

UK (also Ireland and New Zealand): Praia do Flamengo, 284, 2nd floor, Flamengo; tel: 2555-9600.

US: Avenida Presidente Wilson, 147; tel: 3823-2000.

EMERGENCIES

The phone numbers for use in an emergency (*emergência*) are:

Police:	190
Ambulance:	192
Fire:	193

Help!	Socorro!
Call a doctor/the police!	Chame a um médico/a polícia.
I need an English interpreter.	Necesito un intérprete de inglés.

G

GAY AND LESBIAN TRAVELLERS

Rio has long proudly declared itself the gay capital of Latin America. Carnaval is famous for its gay balls and transvestite parades. Many of Brazil's most popular and important singers are openly gay or bisexual, and their adoring public gives the matter little attention. Still, gay people face obstacles in the city, and visitors should not think it the place to lose all sense of proportion and discretion. AIDS continues to ravage Brazilians, and *cariocas* in particular, at a rate that trails only Africa and some parts of Asia. Safe sex should be a commandment.

The gay scene for tourists centres on the Zona Sul (although Lapa also has a very active gay life). The stretch of beach in front of the Copacabana Palace hotel is particularly popular with gay visitors; look for the 'Rainbow' kiosk. (This section of beach is referred to as a *Bolsa*, 'stock market' – ostensibly because it's popular with locals who are looking for rich husbands!) The gay beach in Ipanema is at the end of Rua Farme do Amoedo. Inland, Botafogo has a strong gay presence, especially along rua Visconde de Silva, where you'll find a number of gay restaurants, bars and nightclubs.

The clubs and discos with large gay followings change from season to season; recent favourites include Le Boy and La Girl (Rua Paul Pompeia), The Week (Rua Sacadura Cabral), The Copa (Rua Aires Saldanha) and Dama de Ferro (Rua Vinicius de Moraes). The Gay Ball during Carnaval (Grande Gala G), held at La Scala in Leblon (Avenida Afrânio de Melo Franco, 296), is legendary.

GETTING TO RIO

Air travel. Because of demand, most flights, especially from Europe, go via São Paulo. US gateway cities for travel to Rio include Los Angeles, Miami, Houston, Washington and New York. American Airlines, Continental and United Airlines fly directly to Rio from New York and Miami. From Canada, the gateway city is Toronto. From the UK, flights with British Airways, Tam and Varig depart from London. Most other major European capitals and airlines also serve Rio and, given their close historic relations, the highest number of flights is between Portugal and Brazil with Tap, who from Lisbon offer direct flights not only to Rio and São Paulo but also Brasiliá, Belo Horizonte, Salvador, Recife, Natal and Fortaleza. From Australia and New Zealand, flights originate in Sydney and often stop in Auckland, with connections via Buenos Aires, Santiago or Los Angeles. Flights from Johannesburg, South Africa, stop in São Paulo. Brazil's main international carriers are Varig (<www.varig.com.br>) and Tam (<www.tam.com.br>).

Air Pass. Tam and Varig offer a Brazilian Air Pass for discounted travel within the country. There are several categories of pass available and the rules governing these often change, so check with the airline or your travel agent. You must buy the pass and make the flight reservations before arriving in Brazil. Starting at around US$500, the air pass offers excellent value for money if you will be travelling around the country. The low cost carrier Gol (<www.voegol.com.br>) is another option. Remember, Brazil is considerably larger than Europe.

H

HEALTH AND MEDICAL CARE

Rio, like all of Brazil, is not a great place to get sick, although the private hospitals are excellent. While there is a risk of malaria in certain parts of Brazil, a vacation in Rio holds no special health hazards. You are wise to avoid the tap water, however, and take care that an overdose of sun on the first few days doesn't spoil the rest of your stay.

Most hotels can help put you in contact with doctors who speak English (or French, German or Spanish); you can also ask your consulate for a list of physicians and clinics. Municipal hospitals with round-the-clock emergency rooms include:

Miguel Couto, Rua Bartolomeu Mitre, 1108 (Lagoa); tel: 2274-2121.
Rocha Maia, Rua General Severiano, 91 (Botafogo); tel: 2295-2121.
Souza Aguiar, Praça da República, 111 (Centro); tel: 2295-2295.

Pharmacies and drug stores can be found throughout the city. *Drogarias* sell, among other things, many familiar patent medicines (*remédios*), but only *farmácias* are allowed to fill prescriptions and give injections. The following *farmácias* have a policy of staying open round the clock, seven days a week: Farmácia Piauí, Avenida Ataulfo de Paiva, 1283 (Leblon); Rua Barata Ribeiro, 646 (Copacabana); and Praia do Flamengo, 224 (Flamengo).

Where's the nearest (all-night) pharmacy?	**Onde fica a farmácia (de plantão) mais próxima?**
I need a doctor/dentist.	**Preciso de um médico/dentista.**
an ambulance	**uma ambulância**
hospital	**hospital**
sunburn	**queimadura de sol**
sunstroke	**uma insolação**
a fever	**febre**
stomach ache	**dôr de estômago**

HITCHHIKING

There's no law against it, but hitchhiking in Brazil would not be wise. Don't do it.

HOLIDAYS IN RIO

| 1 January | New Year's Day |
| 20 January | St Sebastian's Feast Day (São Sebastião) |

February/March	Carnaval
March/April	Good Friday/Easter
21 April	Tiradentes
1 May	Labour Day
June	Corpus Christi
7 September	Independence Day (Dia de Independência do Brasil)
12 October	Our Lady of the Apparition
2 November	All Souls' Day
15 November	Proclamation of Brazilian Republic
25 December	Christmas

Carnaval. In the coming years, the dates of Carnaval will be: 20–25 February 2009; 12–17 February 2010; 4–8 March 2011, 17–21 February 2012; and 8–12 February 2013.

L

LANGUAGE

The language of Brazil is Portuguese, not Spanish, so if you say *gracias* instead of *obrigado* to a *carioca*, it's like saying 'thanks' instead of *merci* in Quebec; in effect, you're announcing that you're lumping everybody in South America into the same bag and don't care about local sensibilities – no way to make friends. On the other hand, since Spanish and Portuguese are closely related, you may be able to make some headway if you speak some Spanish (once you've apologised for not knowing any Portuguese!). Even other South Americans, however, find that while Brazilians seem to understand their Spanish, they have great difficulty comprehending responses in Portuguese.

The *Berlitz Portuguese Phrase Book and Dictionary* covers most of the situations you're likely to encounter in Rio, as it gives the Brazilian expressions whenever they differ from the ones used in Portugal. Also useful is the Portuguese-English/English-Portuguese

pocket dictionary, which has a special menu-reader supplement.
Here is a list of useful words and phrases to get you going:

Yes/No	Sim/Não
Please	Por Favor
Thank you	Obrigado/obrigada (fem)
Excuse me/You're welcome	Perdão/De nada
Good morning/Good evening	Bom dia/Boa noite
Good-bye	Adeus/Até lôgo
Do you speak English?	Fala inglês?
I don't speak Portuguese.	Não falo português.
How do you do?	Muito prazer.
How are you?	Como está?
Very well, thank you.	Muito bem, obrigado/ obrigada (fem.)
What does this mean?	Que quer dizer isto?
I don't understand.	Não compreendo.
Please write it down.	Escreva, por favor.
Is there an admission charge?	Paga-se entrada?
Waiter!/Waitress!	Garçon!/Moça!
I'd like…	Queria…/Quero…
How much is that?	Quanto que é isso?
Have you something less expensive?	Tem alguma coisa mas barata?
Just a minute.	Um momento.
What time is it?	Que horas são?
Oops!	Opa!
Help me, please.	Ajude-me, por favor.
where/when/how	onde/quando/como
how long/how far	quanto tempo/ a que distância
yesterday/today/tomorrow	ontem/hoje/amanhã

day/week/month/year	**dia/semana/mês/ano**
left/right	**esquerda/direita**
good/bad	**bom/mau**
big/small	**grande/pequeno**
cheap/expensive	**barato/caro**
hot/cold	**quente/frio**
old/new	**velho/novo**
open/closed	**aberto/fechado**
up/down	**em cima/em baixo**
here/there	**aqui/ali**
free (vacant)/occupied	**livre/ocupado**
easy/difficult	**fácil/difícil**
beach	**praia**

MAPS

The free pamphlets distributed to tourists contain simple maps of Rio. More detailed maps are sold at newsstands. A relatively inexpensive but useful *Mapa Turístico* is published by Geomapas. The easiest map to read is the one included in the *Quatro Rodas Guia do Rio*, also available at newsstands. *Quatro Rodas* is also responsible for the best road maps if you are intending to drive or travel within Brazil.

Where is...?	**Onde fica...?**
I'm lost.	**Estou perdido.**
I'd like a street map of Rio.	**Queria um mapa do Rio.**

MEDIA

The *International Herald Tribune*, *Miami Herald*, *USA Today* and the international editions of *Time* and *Newsweek* are available in hotels and at newsstands. Entertainment listings are found in the Portuguese-language dailies, notably *O Globo* and *Jornal do Brasil*, and the weekly news magazine, *Vejá*. Most hotels have cable, which has CNN and BBC World, as well as other international satellite services.

MONEY

Currency. In an attempt to halt inflation in Brazil, the government pegged the Brazilian currency, the real (R$, plural reais), to the US dollar on its launch in 1994. In 1999 the real was allowed to trade freely against other international currencies. Banknotes: R$1, R$5, R$10, R$50 and R$100; coins: 1, 5, 10, 25 and 50 centavos.

Currency exchange. There are two rates of exchange: the official bank rate and the parallel *(paralelo)* rate, the going exchange on the street, which can be slightly better or worse than the official rate. *Casas de câmbio* are small currency exchange offices and often travel agencies. Your hotel can change money, but at a rate that will probably be worse than the one you can get at *casas de câmbio* or banks. Currency can be changed weekdays at all banks, 10am–4.30pm; *casas de câmbio* are generally open 8am–6pm, Monday to Saturday. Major hotels and some restaurants can change money on Sunday and holidays, but the rate suffers. The best rate is often found at the ATM machines, many of which operate 24 hours. At the end of 2007 the rates were about $1 = R$1.80; €1 = R$2.70; £1 = R$3.80, but travellers should expect to see some instability in exchange rates.

Credit cards. Most major hotels, restaurants, shops and car-hire agencies accept the major credit cards, but there is still little uniformity as to which cards they take. For example, some will take Visa but not MasterCard and vice versa, so if it matters, check first. At many simpler restaurants, credit cards are not accepted.

Travellers' cheques. It is certainly safer to hold your holiday funds in cheques, which can be reclaimed if lost. However, if you do have dollars, and keep them in your hotel safe, you'll find they attract a better rate. It's a good idea to follow instructions given for recording where and when you cashed each cheque.

ATMs. ATM machines – *caixas automáticas* – are widespread and often the safest and best way to get local currency. Not all machines, especially inside banks where there may be many different machines, are linked to the international network, but those that are, are clearly marked, so don't panic if the first machine you try only takes Brazilian cards.

I want to change some dollars/pounds.	**Queria trocar dólares/libras.**
Can you cash a travellers' cheque?	**Pode trocar um cheque de viagem?**
Can I pay with this credit card?	**Posso pagar com este cartão de crédito?**

OPENING HOURS

Many offices and shops have erratic and unpredictable opening and closing hours that defy categorisation. Government offices are usually open weekdays 8am–5pm, but some open as late as 11am and close later in the afternoon. Shops and stores are generally open at least 9am–6pm, but in certain neighbourhoods they have much longer hours, sometimes opening before 8am and closing around 10pm. Shopping centres, like Rio Sul and BarraShopping, open 10am–10pm, except on Sunday when Rio Sul opens at noon and BarraShopping at 3pm. Some businesses close for lunch between noon and 2pm. Some local food stores open Sunday morning. Museums tend to close on Monday. Their weekday hours are 10am or noon to 5 or 6pm; weekends they open 2 or 3pm to 5 or 6pm.

P

POLICE

The emergency telephone number for the police is 190. The police on the street, although they have the duties of municipal police, are members of the military police force (Polícia Militar – PM). The police are patient and courteous with foreigners. If you have a problem, go to one of the many blue-and-white octagonal police posts (marked PM-RIO). The Rio Tourist Police office is in front of the Teatro Casa Grande on Avenida Afrânio de Melo Franco, s/nº in Leblon (tel: 3399-7170).

POST OFFICES

Post offices (correios) are found all over town: look for the yellow sign ECT (Empresa Brasileira de Correios e Telégrafos). The post office at Rio de Janeiro international airport is open 24 hours a day. Branch offices tend to stay open 8am–6pm or 8pm Monday to Friday and 8am–noon on Saturday. It costs about R$2 to send a postcard to either Europe or North America. Service has improved in recent years, but Brazil's correio still leaves much to be desired.

Have you received any mail for...?	**Chegou correspondência para...?**
I'd like a stamp for this letter/this postcard.	**Quero um selo para esta carta/este postal, por favor.**
special delivery (express)	**expresso**
airmail/registered	**via aérea/registrado**

PUBLIC TRANSPORT

Buses. Thousands of city buses race through the streets of Rio when traffic permits; if the traffic is jammed, they race their engines in protest. There are over 400 routes, which might explain why no bus maps of Rio are available. It's best to ask advice on which bus to catch, and where. Avoid rush hours (5–7pm), don't travel by bus after dark, and beware of pickpockets at all times. And hold on for dear life.

You normally enter a city bus through the rear door and leave at the front. A conductor sits near the rear door by a turnstile. For luxury public transport, ride the *frescões* (literally, 'big cool ones'), the air-conditioned buses linking the beach areas with central Rio. The destination is posted in the right-hand front window. On the journey into town, these buses go to the central Menezes Cortês bus station near Praça XV. On the return trip, the destinations cover most of the beach communities from Leme to São Conrado and even beyond. The *frescões* pull over at any bus stop on a signal from a passenger or potential passenger. Buses are also linked to the various Metro stations and can be included in the fare. Details and a map of the bus services linked to the Metro can be found at <www.metrorio.com.br>.

Taxis. Rio's yellow taxis are ubiquitous. There are taxi stands at the airports and at the ferry and railway stations. Except in a rainstorm, the supply of taxis exceeds the demand and they can be hailed at any point. Taxis in Rio are cheap and a much better option for visitors than the buses. As well as the yellow taxis, Rio also has an excellent radio taxi service. The main companies, which can also provide the simplest way to get to the airport, are Cootramo (tel: 3976-9944); Coopertramo (tel: 2209-9292) and Transcoopass (tel: 2209-1555).

Underground. Rio's underground (*Metrô*; <www.metrorio.com.br>) system didn't go into operation until 1979. Early in 1982 15-station Line One was completed, linking the north zone at Praça Saens Peña in Tijuca to the south zone at Botafogo. In recent years new stations have been added to extend the line to Copacabana, Siqueira Campos mid-way along Copacabana, and Cantagalo at the Ipanema end of Copacabana. Special buses link the station at Siqueira Campos with Ipanema, Leblon, Gávea and Barra. The Metro is scheduled to expand its service through to Ipanema at the end of 2009. Line Two links the Line One station at Estácio to Maracanã football stadium and the northern suburbs beyond. Rio's clean, safe, efficient undergound runs from 5am–midnight Monday to Saturday, and on Sunday from 7am–11pm. It is by far the quickest and most comfortable way to get from Copacabana to the city centre.

Tram. Only one tram line still functions in Rio, and it's well worth the trouble, even if only for the nostalgia factor. The terminal is near Largo da *carioca*, and the ancient trams cross the aqueduct high above the Lapa section on the way up to suburban Santa Teresa.

Ferries. Every day more than 150,000 passengers ride the ferries between Rio de Janeiro and Niterói, a 20-minute voyage. Most of them are commuters, who ignore the sea breezes and inspiring views. The ferry costs less than the cheapest city bus. If you're rushed, spend 10 times as much and ride the hydrofoil *(aerobarco)*, which skims across the bay in five minutes. The embarkation point for both ferries and hydrofoils is at Praça XV.

Long-distance buses. Air-conditioned buses, some equipped as sleepers, link Rio with cities as distant as Belém and Buenos Aires. The Novo Rio bus terminal (tel: 3213-1800; <www.novorio.com.br>), centre of all this exotic activity, is in the Santo Cristo district of northern Rio, convenient for the bus drivers but not necessarily for the passengers. There are very frequent buses to São Paulo.

Trains. The main suburban railway station, Estação Dom Pedro II, is just off Avenida Presidente Vargas, the widest street in town. In principle, travel by train is not recommended: the railway station crawls with predators, the journeys seem longer than by bus, prices are higher, and the service is less reliable and less frequent. There are no long-distance passenger train services of note in Brazil. The most picturesque train services in Brazil are Cuirtiba–Paranaguá

(Paraná); Bento Gonçalves–Garibaldi (Rio Grande de Sul); Campinas–Jaguariuna (São Paulo); Tiradentes–São João del Rei (Minas Gerais); and Macapá–Serra do Navio (Amapá).

Air links. About every half hour from 6am–10pm there's a jet flight from Rio's Santos Dumont airport to Congonhas airport near the centre of São Paulo. Several Brazilian airlines operate on the air-bridge *(ponte aérea)*. Santos Dumont has other services, most notably to Brasilia and Belo Horizonte, but the majority of internal flights still go from the international airport.

Where's the nearest bus stop?	**Onde fica a parada de ônibus mais próxima?**
I want a ticket to...	**Queria uma passagem para...**
round-trip (return)	**de ida e volta**
first/second class	**primeira/segunda classe**
Where can I get a taxi?	**Onde posso encontrar um táxi?**
What's the fare to...?	**Quanto custa a corrida para...?**

R

RELIGION

Brazil has the largest Roman Catholic population in the world, but many other religions are active as well. The number of adherents to evangelical Protestant denominations has increased dramatically in recent years, and a number of African religions continue to thrive as well *(see page 80)*. Religious services are regularly held in several languages, including English, French, German, Swedish, Arabic and Chinese.

The monthly booklets issued by the municipal tourism organisation, Riotur, list the times and places for Catholic, Protestant and Jewish services, as well as for the two leading Afro-Brazilian religions, Umbanda and Candomblé.

T

TELEPHONE

Brazil's country code is 55, and the Rio city code is 21. The international service works well. Public telephones are mounted in protective domes commonly called *orelhões* ('big ears'). The orange ones are for local calls, the blue (marked DDD) for long-distance. Phone cards are sold at most newsstands. The number for the operator is 100.

You can dial direct (DDI), which is cheaper, to most countries in the world, by first dialling 00, followed by the long distance operator code (21 for Embratel or 23 for Intelig) and then the country's own code, followed by the area code and the number you want to contact. Should the area code start with a zero, the zero must be dropped. Therefore the number of the Brazilian Embassy in central London, for example, is 00-(21 or 23)-44-20 7399 9000.

When calling from Rio to the rest of Brazil you must also include the code of a long-distance operator, which can be confusing as the Embratel code, 21, is the same as that of the city of Rio.

For operator-assisted, long-distance calls, phone 101; for overseas calls, phone 000-111 or 000-333. Hotels in Rio may allow their guests to make local calls free, but they add a stiff service charge to the tariff for international calls. At the airports and several other key locations, there are public telephone offices from which you can make long-distance and overseas calls. The one in Copacabana, on Avenida N.S. de Copacabana, 540, is open 24 hours; the one in Ipanema, at Rua Visconde Pirajá, 111, is open until midnight.

It is possible to use foreign mobile phones within Brazil, but you should first check with your service provider as to exactly what coverage to expect because it does vary – as does the cost. To dial internationally from a mobile, you may have to follow the same procedure as for a land line and choose a long distance operator. For example 00 (for international) followed by 21 (for Embratel), followed by the number of the country you wish to talk to and the full telephone number.

If you plan to make lots of local calls in Brazil it may be worth getting a Brazilian SIM card for your phone. All main mobile operators in Brazil offer a SIM card-only package and most have stores in the major shopping centres where you can have your phone connected.

If your mobile does not work in Brazil, you can rent a hand set once there. This can be delivered to your hotel or picked up at the airport.

Country codes: Australia 61; Canada 1; Ireland 353; New Zealand 64; South Africa 27; UK 44; US 1.

Can you get me this number in...?	**Pode me ligar este número em...?**
reverse-charge (collect) call	**a cobrar**
person-to-person (personal) call	**pessoa a pessoa**
Where is a public telephone?	**Onde tem um orelhão?**

TIME ZONES

Rio Standard Time is 3 hours behind Greenwich Mean Time. During Brazilian summer (Nov–Feb), the clock is advanced 1 hour in Rio.

	Los Angeles	New York	**Rio**	London	Sydney
January:	7am	9am	**noon**	2pm	1am
July:	9am	11am	**noon**	4pm	1am

TIPPING

A 10 percent service charge is generally included in restaurant bills. If not, that amount should be left for acceptable service. For bellboys on errands, the odd coin is appropriate. Taxi drivers do not receive tips so round up the fare. Some further guidelines, in dollar equivalents:

Hotel porter, per bag	US$1
Maid, per week	US$10
Tour guide	US$3–$5

TOILETS

Public conveniences are rare in Rio, but you can always find facilities in hotels, restaurants and bars. There's no problem walking in to a bar or restaurant just to use the facilities. If there's an attendant on duty, a tip is expected. Ladies is *Senhoras* or *Damas*; Gentlemen is *Homens* or, sometimes, *Cavalheiros*. Signs are often abbreviated to 'S' and 'H' ('She' and 'He', if you forget).

| Where are the toilets? | **Onde ficam os toiletes?** |

TOURIST INFORMATION

For further information about Rio prior to your trip the best source is now the internet (see WEBSITES) or specialised tour operators.

For tourist information once you have arrived in Brazil, contact one of the following:

Riotur (city tourism authority): Praça Pio X 119, 9°, Centro; tel: 2271-7000/2271-7048; <www.rio.rj.gov.br/riotur/en/home.php>.
TurisRio (covering the State of Rio de Janeiro): Rua da Ajuda 5, 6°, Centro; tel: 2215-0011; <www.turisrio.rj.gov.br>.

Pamphlets and information can also be obtained at the Riotur booths at the international airport (6am–11pm); in Copacabana, Avenida Princesa Isabel, 183; tel: 2541-7522 (open: Mon–Fri 9am–6pm); or at the arrival section of the Rodoviário Novo Rio bus terminal; tel: 2263-4857 (open: 6am–8pm).

TOUR OPERATORS

Due to the fact that South America has not been a mainstream tourist destination for US and European travellers, the tour operators who do specialise in the region tend to be very knowledgeable and can help put together the best programmes and most complex itineraries, whether you are just visiting Rio or touring the whole of Brazil. It does not even matter if you haven't purchased your air ticket from them.

In the UK, all the best tour operators to Brazil are members of the Latin American Travel Association (LATA) and are listed on the association's website (<www.lata.org>). A list of UK operators can also be found on the Brazilian Embassy website (<www.brazil. org. uk>) and the same is true of US operators who are listed on the Brazilian Embassy website in Washington (<www.braziltourism. org>). The US equivalent of LATA is the Brazilian Tour Operators Association (BTOA; <www.braziltouroperators.com>).

W

WEBSITES

www.accorhotels.com.br Brazil's largest hotel and apart-hotel chain
www.bondinho.com.br About Sugar Loaf
www.brasilemb.org Brazilian Embassy in Washington
www.brazil.org.uk, www.braziltourism.org Brazilian Tourist Office
www.braziltour.com Embratur, Brazilian Tourist Authority
www.buziosdirect.com Búzios accommodation
www.buziosonline.com.br Búzios tourist information, including hotels and *pousadas*
www.buziosturismo.com Búzios accommodation
www.camaecafe.com.br Cama e Café (bed-and-breakfast)
www.corcovado.com.br The Corcovado funicular
www.maracana.rj.gov.br Maracanã football stadium
www.metrorio.com.br Metro services
www.paraty.com.br Paratay tourist information
www.petropolis.rj.gov.br/fctp/geral_turismo/index.htm Petrópolis tourist information
www.riodejaneiro-turismo.com.br Riotur (Rio tourist office)
http://shuttlerio.com.br/br Airport Shuttle
www.turisrio.rj.gov.br TurisRio (tourist office for the state of Rio)

Recommended Hotels

Most visitors to Rio wish to stay near the beach which is where most of the luxury hotels are located, in the Zona Sul. But good deals can also be had just a block or two away from the beach. A beach view may cost as much as 25 percent more than a room without one. There are good budget hotels in the suburbs of Glória, Flamengo and Botafogo and they can even be found in Copacabana and Ipanema.

High season in Rio coincides with summer in the southern hemisphere, roughly from mid-December through Carnaval (late February to mid-March). Advance reservations are necessary during high season, especially at Carnaval and the New Year. Whatever time of year you travel to Rio, and as independent as you may be as a traveller, have at least your first night in Rio pre-booked so you have a base to head for on arrival. While most visitors tend to go for hotels in Copacabana and Ipanema, the first new hotels are starting to open up in Barra da Tijuca.

As a basic guide, the symbols below have been used to indicate high-season rates in US dollars, based on double occupancy with bath/shower. Hotels listed take major credit cards unless otherwise stated.

$$$$$	above $250
$$$$	$175–$250
$$$	$125–$175
$$	$75–$125
$	below $75

RIO

CENTRO

Guanabara Palace $$$ *Av. Presidente Vargas, 392, tel: 2195-6000, fax: 2516-1582, <www.windsorhoteis.com>.* One of Rio's most traditional city-centre hotels, and one of the largest, was completely refurbished in 2003 and is the best choice for travellers wanting to stay in the historic centre away from the beach. The Guanabara Palace sits on Rio's widest avenue, opposite the Candelaria Church.

Rooftop bar with a deck. Wheelchair access. 383 rooms. Guanabara's only rival in the city centre is its sister hotel, the 350-room Serrador Palace which is located on the edge of Cinelandia with views across the bay to Sugar Loaf.

GLÓRIA/FLAMENGO/LAPA

Cama e Café $–$$ *(various locations in Lapa), tel: 2224-5689, <www.camaecafe.com.br>*. One of the great innovations in 2003 was the birth of Cama e Café, an organisation for the historic houses in the Lapa district that offer bed-and-breakfast accommodation and sometimes more. Cama e Café has more than 50 houses on its books, many of which belong to the artists who have their studios in Lapa. There is even an historic convent on the books.

Hotel Flórida $$ *Rua Ferreira Viana, 81, Flamengo, tel: 2195-6800, fax: 2285-5777, <www.windsorhoteis.com>*. One of the older and more dependable budget establishments. Rooms have parquet floors and nice bathrooms. A swimming pool was built in the early 1990s during an overall refurbishment. A block from Flamengo beach and next to the Metrô station, this hotel is very popular in high season. 312 rooms.

Hotel Glória $$$ *Rua do Russel, 63, Glóriam, tel: 2555-7272, fax: 2555-7282, <www.hotelgloriario.com.br>*. Once the grandest beachfront hotel in Brazil, the Glória lost its beach to landfill when the tunnel to Zona Sul was built. Still, it's a classic. Favoured by tour groups and business travellers due to its proximity to central Rio. Guest rooms, refurbished in the mid-1990s, have Brazilian antiques. Wheelchair access. 630 rooms make it the largest hotel in Rio.

Hotel Turístico $ *Ladeira da Glória, 30, Glória, tel: 2557-7698, fax: 2558-5815*. One of the more popular basic budget establishments, the Túristico is well-situated, right by the Glória Metrô stop. You'll always find a crowd of European and American backpacker types. Rooms (with small balconies) and services are functional. 47 rooms.

COPACABANA/LEME

Copacabana Palace $$$$$ *Av. Atlântica, 1702, tel: 2548-7070, fax: 2235-7330, <www.copacabanapalace.com.br>*. Long the standard-bearer for luxury (and symbol of Rio), the regal Copacabana Palace hasn't slipped. The most elegant hotel in the city, and part of the Orient-Express group, the Copa has very tastefully decorated rooms, great views, an elegant pool and two excellent restaurants. The executive business floor is exceptional. Advance booking a must. Wheelchair access. 222 rooms.

Excelsior $$$$ *Av. Atlântica, 1800, tel: 2195-5800, fax: 2257-1850, <www.windsorhoteis.com>*. Totally refurbished at the end of the 1990s by the Windsor Hotel group, this is an excellent option for business or leisure travellers who can't afford the very top hotels. Location is excellent, being on the beachfront in the same block as the Copacabana Palace. Small rooftop pool. 233 rooms.

Iberostar Grand Hotel Copacabana $$$$$ *Av. Atlântica, 1020, tel: 3873-8888, fax: 3873-8777, <www.iberostar.com.br>*. For over three decades Le Mériden operated this landmark hotel, ideally located at the closest point of Copacabana to the city centre. In 2007 it was taken over by the Spanish Iberostar Group which has totally refurbished the property to guarantee its position as one of Rio's premiere establishments. 496 rooms.

JW Marriott $$$$$ *Av. Atlântica, 2600, tel: 2545-6500, fax: 2545-6555, <www.marriott.com>*. A modern hotel on the Copacabana beachfront, offering exactly what clients of this worldwide group expect, especially business travellers. Voted one of the 'Best Hotels in Latin America' by the US readers of *Conde Nast Traveler*. Small rooftop pool and excellent fitness centre. Worth paying extra for a beachfront room. 245 rooms.

Luxor Regente Hotel $$$ *Av. Atlântica, 3716, tel: 2525-2070, fax: 2267-7693, <www.luxor-hotels.com>*. Overlooking the beach, near the Ipanema end of Copacabana. The largest of three Luxor properties, the Regente is a solid and reasonably priced luxury hotel.

A bit labyrinthine, it has a business centre, tiny pool and health club on the top floor. Service is very professional. 236 rooms.

Miramar Palace $$$ *Av. Atlântica, 3668, tel: 2195-6200, fax: 2521-3294, <www.windsorhoteis.com>.* Situated at the Ipanema end of Copa beach. Rooms have good views of the fort and docked fishing boats. Service is friendly. There's a glassed-in café/bar on the lobby floor, and a rooftop bar with a deck. Wheelchair access. 150 rooms.

Ouro Verde $$ *Av. Atlântica, 1456, tel: 2543-4123, fax: 2543-4776, <www.dayrell.com.br>.* Once one of Rio's great hotels, and one of the world's first boutique hotels when it opened in 1950, the standards have somewhat slipped at the Ouro Verde. The hotel, which is a listed building, remains intimate and refined, however; large rooms are tastefully decorated, many with nice balconies, and offer good value overall. Wheelchair access. 64 rooms.

Pestana Rio Atlântica $$$$ *Av. Atlântica, 2964, tel: 2548-6332, fax: 2255-6410, <www.pestana.com>.* Modern 18-floor hotel, smack on Copacabana's beachfront avenue. The well-designed hotel, popular with both business travellers and families, has a Brazilian flavour. Half of the tiled rooms are suites and all have balconies. The hotel has a rooftop pool, excellent health club, and even a small cinema. Part of the Portuguese Pestana group. Wheelchair access. 217 rooms.

Porto Bay Rio Internacional $$$$ *Av. Atlântica, 1500, tel: 2546-8000, fax: 2542-5443, <www.riointernacional.com.br>.* Built in the mid-1990s and refurbished in 2007, the polished Internacional is popular with business travellers and holidaymakers. The business centre is one of the city's best. The elegant rooms are spacious and have great balconies and beach views. Its sister hotel is the Porto Bay Glenzhaus in Búzios. Rooftop pool, fitness centre and restaurant. 116 rooms.

Rio Othon Palace & Othon Hotels $$$$ *Av. Atlântica, 3264, tel: 2106-1500, fax: 2522-1697, <www.othonhotels.com>.* This high-rise, hugely popular with tour groups, seems to have been around forever. Rooms are tastefully decorated. The hotel has a rooftop pool and a fine gym. Wheelchair access. 586 rooms. Note: The Othon group is one of the largest and most traditional hotel groups in Brazil. In Copacabana, the chain offers five hotels of varying degrees of sophistication, four of which are on the beachfront, making them ideal for watching or participating in the New Year celebrations.

Sofitel Rio $$$$$ *Av. Atlântica, 4240, tel: 2525-1232, fax: 2525-1200, <www.sofitel.com>.* This classic luxury hotel was purchased and totally renovated by the French Accor group in the late 1990s to the highest standards. Opened by Frank Sinatra in 1979, it has a superb location at the end of Copacabana closest to Ipanema, across from the fort; the views over the whole sweep of Copacabana are stupendous. There are two pools. The restaurant, Le Pré Catelan, is one of Rio's best. Wheelchair access. 388 rooms.

IPANEMA/LEBLON

Caesar Park $$$$$ *Av. Vieira Souto, 460, tel: 2525-2525, fax: 2521-6000, <www.caesarpark-rio.com>.* Ipanema's best, along with the Fasano, this top-flight, luxury hotel is preferred by business travellers (the hotel will even provide you with a laptop, fax and printer) as well as Madonna, and the Japanese, Spanish and Swedish royal families. The 45-sq m (488-sq ft) Imperial Suite is one of Rio's best. Rooms are elegant and ample, service excellent. Private security watches over guests on the beach and there is also a small rooftop pool. Breakfast, on the top floor overlooking Ipanema and Corcovado, is a standout. Wheelchair access. 228 rooms.

Everest Rio Hotel $$$$ *Rua Prudente de Morais, 1117, tel: 2525-2200, fax: 2521-3198, <www.everest.com.br>.* The location is excellent: just a block from the beach behind Caesar Park, it's surrounded by Ipanema's restaurants, bars and boutiques. Rooms feature large windows; the views from the rooftop deck and the Grill 360° Restaurant take in Corcovado. Though popular with business travellers, there is a play area well suited for families. 156 rooms. Nearby is the 25-room Everest Park Hotel, a less expensive member of the same chain.

Fasano $$$$$ *Av. Vieira Souto, 80, tel: 3202-4000, fax: 3202-4010, <www.fasano.com.br>.* There was a huge amount of expectation when Fasano finally opened its doors at the end of 2007. It has not disappointed and is Rio's most stylish and sophisticated boutique hotel offering an eclectic mix of tastes and styles. Located at the Copacabana end of Ipanema beach, Fasano's bar (Baretto) and Italian seafood restaurant (Fasano Al Mare) are two of Rio's most sought-after spots. The rooftop deck and pool, with fabulous views over Ipanema, are for the guests only. 92 rooms.

Ipanema Plaza $$$$ *Rua Farme de Amoedo 34, 4240, tel: 3687-2000, fax: 3687-2001, <www.ipanemaplaza.com.br>.* Located one block back from Ipanema beach, this hotel is a favourite with travellers preferring tranquil and sophisticated Ipanema to Copacabana. Stylish and modern. Rooftop pool. Wheelchair access. 140 rooms.

Marina All Suites $$$$ *Av. Delfim Moreira, 696, tel: 2172-1100, fax: 2294-1644, <www.marinaallsuites.com.br>.* The finest hotel on the Leblon end of the beach. Rooms, as the name suggests, are suites and the top eight have been decorated by celebrated Brazilian designers, making this one of the city's few boutique hotels. The 360-degree views from the rooftop pool are excellent (Gávea mountain is very close). The bistro restaurant, with ocean views, is recommended. 38 rooms. Close by is the more traditional Marina Palace Hotel (<www.hotel-marina.com.br>), which is another fine option, with 150 rooms.

Praia Ipanema & Sol Ipanema $$$ *Av. Vieira Souto, 706/320, tel: 2540-4949 (Praia), 2525-2020 (Sol), fax: 2239-6889 (Praia), 2247-8484 (Sol), <www.praiaipanema.com.br>, <www.solipanema.com>.* These unremarkable hotels' location on Ipanema beach, only shared by the much more expensive Caesar Park and Fasano, makes them excellent value for any travellers or families coming to Rio to enjoy the city. Also close to many of Rio's best restaurants and bars in Ipanema.

VIDIGAL/SÃO CONRADO

Inter-Continental Rio $$$$$ *Rua Prefeito Mendes de Morais, 222, tel: 3323-2200, fax: 33323-5500, <www.ichotelsgroup.com>.* In São Conrado, bordered by the beach, the Gávea Golf Club and the Fashion Mall, Rio's Inter-Continental is a true resort hotel, or as much of a resort as you can get in a metropolitan city. Popular with American groups, the 'Inter' has tennis courts, multiple swimming pools and good restaurants. The Inter-Continental is also well located for events at Riocentro and for business travellers working with businesses located in Barra. It was totally renovated in 2004. 431 rooms.

Sheraton Rio Hotel & Towers $$$$$ *Av. Niemeyer, 121, tel: 2274-1122, fax: 2239-5643, <www.sheraton-rio.com>.* The only hotel directly on a beach, this first-rate, luxury resort has tennis courts, two pools, a great gym and three restaurants with ocean views. Perfect for relaxed privacy, but still close to Leblon's restaurants and clubs. Sheraton guards patrol the beach regularly. 'Tower' apartments are excellent. Wheelchair access. 617 rooms.

BARRA DA TIJUCA

Sheraton Barra Hotel & Suites $$$$ *Av. Lúcio Costa, 3150, tel: 3139-8000, fax: 3139-8085, <www.sheraton-barra.com.br>.* Reflecting the growing importance of Barra da Tijuca in the life of Rio, a number of serious hotels have started to spring up along the beachfront to cater mainly for Brazilians and other South Americans who want to be in the heart of 'new' Rio. Leading the pack is the Sheraton Barra Hotel & Suites, a five-star property offering 292 well-equipped rooms and suites all with ocean views and balconies. The hotel has a good pool area, fitness centre, and sits right in front of Barra beach. Closest of the major hotels to Riocentro, the city's main convention and conference centre. Wheelchair access.

ANGRA DOS REIS

Blue Tree Angra $$$$$ *Estrada Benedito Adelino, 8413, tel: (024) 3379-2800, fax: (024) 3379-2801, <www.bluetree.com.br>.* Blue Tree is the leading operator of high-class resorts in Brazil, and their property in Angra, 160km (100 miles) from Rio, is ideal for those travellers looking for a full resort experience close to Rio. As well as the facilities you might expect of a top resort, the hotel, which is located in a preserved area of Atlantic rainforest, offers excellent walks and treks. It is located on its own beach with views of Angra Bay. 319 rooms.

Pestana Angara $$$$ *Estrada Benedito Adelino, 3700, tel: (024) 3364-2005, fax: (024) 3365-1909, <www.pestana.com>.* Luxurious and romantic getaway close to Angra, with individual bungalows strategically placed in the grounds around a central pool, restaurant and bar complex. Memorable views across Angra Bay to the Atlantic rainforest. 27 bungalows.

PARATY

Pousada do Ouro $$ *Rua Dr Pereira, 145, tel: (024) 3371-4300, fax: (024) 3371-1311, <www.pousadaouro.com.br>.* This handsome *pousada* in Paraty's historic centre was used in the film *Gabriela*. It has attractive rooms, safes, saunas, a smart common area, and a good-sized room for business meetings. Breakfast included. 26 rooms.

Pousada Porto Imperial $$$ *Rua Tenente Francisco Antônio, tel: (024) 3371-2323, fax: (024) 3371-2111, <www.pousadaportoparaty. com.br>.* One of the largest *pousadas* in the historic centre (near the river, behind the Igreja dos Remédios), this place has more facilities than any other lodging in Paraty. Its attractive rooms are all named after famous women; there's a pool, tennis court, business meeting room, and a lovely patio and gardens. Breakfast included. 44 rooms. The hotel also operates the nearby Marina Porto Imperial, one of the largest and best-equipped marinas in the region.

BÚZIOS

Byblos $$$ *Morro do Humaitá, 8, tel: (022) 2623-1162, fax: (024) 2623-2828, <www.pousadabyblos.com.br>.* One of the original *pousadas* in the area, Byblos maintains high standards. It sits on a hill overlooking Armação and Ossos beaches and is a 5-minute walk from Rua das Pedras. Decktop pool. Breakfast included. 21 rooms.

Casas Brancas $$$$ *Morro do Humaitá, 10, tel: (022) 2623-1458, fax: (024) 2623-2147, <www.casasbrancas.com.br>.* Not only one of the most picturesque *pousadas* in Búzios, but also one of the most luxurious. Popular with visitors looking for something special. Excellent service. Decktop pool. 32 rooms.

Hibiscus Beach $$ *Praia João Fernandes, tel/fax: (022) 2623-6221, <www.hibiscusbeach.com.br>*. Hibiscus Beach consists of individual bungalows, and is located above João Fernandes beach. It has its own swimming pool located in the peaceful, tropical garden. Good for families or couples. Unusually, it is British owned and managed, yet retains a distinctly Búzios charm. 13 rooms.

Pousada do Martin Pescador $$$ *Enseada do Gancho, 15, tel: (022) 2623-1449, fax: (022) 2623-2547, <www.martin-pescador. com.br>*. Beautifully situated, it hugs the hills above Manguinhos beach. Beds are elevated so that the view from one's pillow is of the bay. There's a congenial common area and a squash court and pool area. The sauna comes with a view of the sea. Breakfast is included. 18 rooms.

Le Relais La Borie $$$ *Geriba Beach, tel: (022) 2620-8504, fax: (022) 2623-2303, <www.laborie.com.br>*. This delightful *pousada*, located directly on Geriba beach, is one of the largest and best equipped on the Búzios peninsula. Restaurant, two bars, two pools and an indoor jacuzzi. 38 rooms.

VALE DO PARAÍBA

Fazenda Arvoredo $$$ *Barra do Piraí, RJ, tel/fax: (024) 2447-2001, <www.hotelarvoredo.com.br>*. This large and lovely former coffee plantation dates from the middle of the 19th century. The immaculate rooms, all identical, are located in former slaves' quarters. Situated on 460 hectares (1,140 acres), with opportunities for hiking, biking and horse-riding. The *fazenda* also has a large pond for rowing boats, and a rustic pool. Meals included. 33 rooms.

Fazenda Ponte Alta $$$ *Parque Santana, Barra do Piraí, RJ, tel/fax: (024) 2443-5159, <www.pontealta.com.br>*. Fronted by giant palm trees and a stable, this beautiful coffee estate is perfect if you want to immerse yourself in Brazilian history. Rooms are all different; some are in the lovely main house, others across the garden in former slaves' quarters *(senzala)*. Pool. All meals included. Nine rooms.

Recommended Restaurants

Much of the Rio dining scene is concentrated in the Zona Sul; Ipanema and Leblon in particular have a large array of desirable restaurants. Reservations are usually only necessary at the top and most fashionable restaurants. Almost all restaurants are casual, even the most exclusive. Don't overlook some of the simpler bar/restaurants, called *botequims* – they are an authentic slice of Rio life; for the *carioca*, the equivalent of the British pub. Suffice to say it is difficult to eat badly in Rio and eating out should be seen as another of the city's many attractions. Below is only a small cross section of what Rio has to offer.

The price symbols are intended as a guide only, and are based on a standard three-course meal for one. Prices are given in US dollars due to the fluctuation in the real.

$$$$$	above $50
$$$$	$25–$50
$$$	$15–$25
$$	$10–$15
$	below $10

RIO

CENTRO

Bar Luiz $$ *Rua da Carioca, 39, tel: 2262-6900.* Open Mon–Sat, 11am–11pm. One of the city's oldest surviving restaurants, this *botequim* has hosted a long roster of illustrious *cariocas*. Founded in 1887, it moved to its present location near the Largo da Carioca in 1927. The dining room has simple tables, white tablecloths and photos of old Rio. The menu is German.

Cais do Oriente $$$$ *Rua Visconde de Itaboraí, 8, tel: 2203-0178, <www.caisdooriente.com.br>.* Open Tues–Sat noon–midnight, Sun–Mon noon–4pm. Located in a listed warehouse built in 1878, close to the docks and city centre, this large establishment is spread over three floor and offers a real mix of atmospheres and cuisines where east meets west and Brazil meets the Orient. Bar has live shows. An interesting choice when sightseeing in the city centre.

SANTA TERESA

Adega do Pimenta $$ *Rua Alm. Alexandrino, 296, tel: 2224-7554.* Open Mon, Wed–Fri 11.30am–10pm, Sat–Sun, 11am 6pm. This hole-in-the-wall is a slice of Bavaria in old Santa Teresa. German food is not only the speciality, it's all you'll find: bratwurst, sauerkraut, potato salad and German cold cuts. Wash them down with cold beer – light or dark, the latter a rarity in Rio.

Aprazível Sabor $$$$$ *Rua Aprazível, 62, tel: 2507-7334.* Open Thur–Sat for lunch and dinner, Sun 1–6pm. This small French restaurant in an old house is one of the most fashionable in Rio. It attracts the chic and the politically connected. Both classic and innovative French dishes, all meticulously prepared.

Bar do Arnaudo $ *Rua Alm. Alexandrino, 316, tel: 2210-0817.* Open Tues–Sat noon–10pm, Sun 11am–8.30pm. This tiny, family-run restaurant serves authentic cooking from northeast Brazil. Huge portions should be shared. Best are sun-dried salty meats, served with *farofa* (fried manioc flour) and rice and beans. Complement the spicy food with a *batida* (fruit shake) or cold beer.

GLÓRIA, CATETE, FLAMENGO AND BOTAFOGO

Adega do Valentim $$$$ *Rua da Passagem, 176, Botafogo, tel: 2295-2748.* Open daily noon–1am. Tucked away on a side street in Botafogo, this classic Portuguese restaurant has many *carioca* devotees. It exudes rich Old World atmosphere. If you're not familiar with Portuguese cooking, this is a good place to try it. Flavoursome grilled salmon and spicy rabbit are among the mainstays, as well as bacalhau dishes based on traditional dried salt cod.

Café Lamas $$ *Rua Marquês de Abrantes, 18, tel: 2556-0799.* Open daily 9.30am–2.50am. One of the oldest restaurants in Rio, Café Lamas is an institution. President Getúlio Vargas ate here, and the celebrated writer Machado de Assis was a regular. Founded in 1874, its decor is simple and service very professional. The menu is traditional, focusing on meat. A classic dish is the Lamas steak.

Porcão's Rio $$$ *Aterro do Flamengo, tel: 3389-8989.* Open daily noon–1am. Flagship establishment of one of Rio's best value *rodízio* barbecues. Excellent cuts of meat keep coming, but they compete with seafood, and sushi buffet dishes and a splendid salad bar. The setting, in the centre of Flamengo Park, has spectacular views over Sugar Loaf and Corcovado.

COPACABANA/LEME

Cipriani $$$$$ *Av. Atlântica, 1702, tel: 2545-8747.* Open daily noon–midnight. This elegant restaurant in the Copacabana Palace hotel overlooks the cinematic pool, which, illuminated at night, evokes the glamour of the 1920s. The northern Italian cuisine is extremely well executed. The decor is plush. For a special place to dine, it's good value. One of Rio's, if not South America's, best.

Marius $$$$ *Av. Atlântica, 290, tel: 2104-9002.* Open daily noon–midnight. In Leme, overlooking the beach, this high-class *churrascaria* has for 20 years been one of the top places in Rio to gorge on grilled meats – nearly 40 different types circulate before your eyes. The terrific salad bar has vegetables culled from a private garden.

Le Pré Catelan $$$$ *Av. Atlântica, 4240, tel: 2525-1160.* Open Mon–Sat 7pm–midnight. Traditionally one of Rio's finest restaurants which is now back to its best. Since 2003 the influential weekly magazine, *Vejá*, has judged it to be one of the city's best French restaurants. Located in the Sofitel Rio.

Siri Mole & Cia $$$ *Rua Francisco Otaviano, 50, tel: 2267-0894.* Open daily noon–midnight, dinner only on Monday. *Cariocas* adore this place, which serves Brazilian food in an elegant and fashionable setting. The emphasis is on seafood, and a standout is *moqueca de camarão* (shrimp stew). The namesake dish is soft crabs. Old-fashioned coffee is a highlight. One of the city's best Brazilian restaurants.

IPANEMA

Bar Bofetada $ *Rua Farme de Amoedo, 87, tel: 2227-1675*. Open daily. This bar/restaurant in the heart of Ipanema has lots of character. The outdoor tables are preferred by regulars. Specialities include *caldinha de feijão* (bean broth) and *Romário x Túlia* (jerked beef with cassava). Live *chorinho* music Monday at 0pm.

Casa da Feijoada $$ *Rua Prudente de Morais, 10, tel: 2247-2776*. Open daily. The slogan – and reality – at this restaurant is 'Every day is a day for *feijoada*'. This long-standing, small and simple restaurant is right next to the Ipanema square that hosts the Hippie Fair every Sunday. The national dish, *feijoada*, is a must, athough the menu includes other classic Brazilian dishes, such as *moqueca*.

Fasano al Mare $$$$$ *Av. Vieira Souto, 80, tel: 3202 4000*. Open daily noon–1am. Stylish Italian seafood restaurant located in the Fasano Hotel on Ipanema beachfront. Like its sister restaurant, Gero, Fasano Al Mare is one of the most sought-after eateries for the city's in-crowd. Not cheap, but an experience in good living and one of Rio's best.

Gero $$$$$ *Rua Anibal de Mendonça, 157, tel: 2239-8158*. Open daily noon–1am. When it opened in 2002, Gero became an instant hit with those who matter in artistic, financial and political circles as it came with an impressive pedigree, being owned by the Fasano family, who are also responsible for the talked-about boutique hotel opened in late 2007. Gero's menu offers an interesting mix of classical and innovative dishes. A treat for business or pleasure, but reservations remain a must.

Gula Gula $$$ *Rua Henrique Dumont, 57, tel: 2259-3084, <www.gulagula.com.br>*. Open daily noon–midnight. There are 12 Gula Gulas spread across Rio and all ooze *carioca* charm in much the same way as bossa nova. The most relaxed, and at the same time most fashionable, is the Ipanema branch, located just one block back from the beach. Excellent value for money given the quality of setting, cuisine and service.

Manoel & Juaquim $ *Rua Barão da Torre, 162, tel: 2522-1863.* Open daily 5pm–2am. A lively and informal *botequim* that has. emerged as a local favourite, and the bar in particular has attracted a dedicated following. Crab is prominent on the menu: try crab soup, pastries, crab pizza or, on Tuesday, the Crab Stravaganza. (You can also get chicken if that's too much crab for you.) Other branches of Manoel & Juaquim can be found in Copacabana, Lapa and Largo do Machado in Flamengo.

New Natural $ *Rua Barão da Torre, 173, tel: 2287-0301.* Open daily. A handsome *lanchonete*, where the emphasis is on simple and well-prepared vegetarian fare. The same owners operate a natural foods shop next door. No credit cards.

Plataforma $$$ *Rua Adalberto Ferreira, 32, tel: 2274-4022.* Open daily noon–midnight. This *churrascaria* attracts huge numbers of tourists to its giant dining room. At night there's a samba spectacular upstairs. Dine on meat until your heart is content and your cholesterol level soars into the danger zone.

Porcão $$$ *Rua Barão da Torre, 218, tel: 2522-0999.* Open daily 11am–1am. One of Rio's best *rodízio* barbecue houses. Excellent cuts of meat keep coming, but they compete with seafood buffet dishes and a splendid salad bar. Though the name translates as 'Big Pig', the setting is more elegant than most similarly priced *rodízios*.

Satyricon $$$$ *Rua Barão da Torre, 192, tel: 2521-0627.* Open daily, dinner only on Monday. The fine Italian menu emphasises fresh fish and shellfish. A favourite of stars and business magnates, it features a sushi bar and an attention-getting dining room. One of Rio's most reliable for over 25 years.

Yemanjá $$ *Rua Visconde de Pirajá, 128, tel: 2247-7004.* Open Mon–Fri 6pm–11.30pm, Sat–Sun noon–midnight. Brazilian food with a distinct Bahaian flavour is served at this classy restaurant tucked in among clothing and film shops. Named for the goddess of the sea, this is a good place to order fish, especially shrimp and fish *moquecas* (stews).

LEBLON

Antiquarius $$$$$ *Rua Aristides Espinola, 19, tel: 2294-1049.* Open daily noon–2am. This small and elegant spot has been serving exquisitely prepared classic Portuguese dishes for over 30 years. The clientele can be gauged by the Mercedes and BMWs with bored drivers waiting outside. The ambiance, though, is unpretentious. Upstairs, antiques are for sale, hence the name.

Bar Bracarense $ *Rua José Linhares, 85, tel: 2294-3549.* Open daily 7am–11pm. Named 'best bar in Rio', Bracarense is always buzzing with people having a *chopp* (beer) and a snack, such as the *bacalhão* (codfish) and shrimp and cassava balls. In summer, it's a popular gathering spot after the beach. Lifelong customers maintain ever-escalating tabs. No credit cards.

Carlota $$ *Rua Dias Ferreira, 64, tel: 2540-6821.* Open Tues–Fri 7pm–midnight, Sat 1–5.30pm, 7pm–1am, Sun 1–11pm. Cosy bistro with an innovative menu that has made it one of Rio's most sought-out restaurants. Nice *carioca* feel.

Celeiro $$ *Rua Dias Ferreira, 199, tel: 2274-7843.* Open Mon–Sat 10am–5pm. This attractive restaurant on Leblon's major restaurant row is 'a quilo' – a place where you pay by weight. The simple, light fare includes salads, sandwiches and quiches; the salad bar will delight vegetarians and non-veggies alike. The outdoor tables are popular with young people.

Doce Delicia $$ *Av. Afrânio de Melo Franco, 290, tel: 2512-6549.* Open daily 11.30am–midnight. This spot lives up to its name: Delicious Sweets. If you have a sweet tooth, don't miss the delectable *creme de maracujá* (passion fruit cream pie) or one of the other amazing cakes and pies. It's also a reliable place for lunch or dinner (as a prelude to dessert, of course). Light dishes include quiches and croquettes; for a larger meal try filet mignon, pasta or the dish of the day.

Espaço Brasa Leblon $$$$ *Av. Afrânio de Melo Franco, 131, tel: 2111-5700.* Located across the road from Shopping Leblon, Espaço

Brasa Leblon is one of the largest (400 seats) and smartest of the *rodízio*-style barbecue houses. The restaurant specialises in meats but also offers a large, diverse buffet and a wide variety of salads and seafood, including giant prawns and oysters. Something for every taste.

Garcia & Rodrigues $$ *Av. Ataulfo de Paiva, 1251, tel: 3206-4100.* Open daily 8am–midnight. This charming establishment is part of a Rio trend: part coffee shop and bakery, part restaurant. You can have breakfast downstairs, selecting from the assortment of breads and croissants, while the simple international menu upstairs is ideal for lunch.

Giuseppe Grill $$$$ *Av. Bartolomeu Mitre, 370, tel: 2249-3055.* Open daily noon–4pm, 7pm–midnight. Arguably Rio's most stylish and sophisticated steak house, serving some of the city's best steaks and grills. The house also boasts an excellent wine list. The original Giuseppe Grill is located downtown at Rua Sete de Setembro, 65, and is just as popular as the Leblon branch for business lunches.

Jobi $ *Av. Ataulfo de Paiva, 1166, tel: 2274-0547.* Open daily 9am–4.30am. Lots of locals stop by for a nightcap here, but it's also a good place for a meal. Specialities include *caldinha de feijão* (bean broth), jerked beef and *feijoada*. When there's a football match on TV, be prepared for a true Brazilian experience.

Pizzaria Guanabara $ *Av. Ataulfo de Paiva, 1228, tel: 2294-0797.* Open daily. The famous Guanabara is one of Rio's classic pizzarias, open late and often busy until it closes. It's popular with artists and old-school *carioca* bohemians.

Tower Grill $$$ *Shopping Leblon, Av. Afrânio de Melo Franco, 290, tel: 3138-8633.* Open daily noon–midnight. The Tower Grill in the Rio Sul Shopping centre has proved itself as one of the city's most reliable steak houses. The latest branch, located on the top floor of Shopping Leblon, offers the same high standards of cuisine but also benefits from spectacular views across the Lagoa to Corcovado. The restaurant is on the same floor as Kinoplex Leblon, one of Rio's most modern and well-equipped cinema complexes.

LAGOA/JARDIM BOTÂNICO

Bar Lagoa $$ *Av. Epitácio Pessoa, 1675, tel: 2523-1135.* Open daily 6pm–2am, Sat–Sun noon–2pm. This charming 1934 *botequim* has an art deco interior and a nice veranda facing the lagoon. It's great for lunch or dinner, but late in the evening is when things really get going – and noisy. The fare is German, such as *Kussler Rippchen* (ribs) *mit Sauerkraut,* and bratwurst with potato salad, backed by international favourites. Portions are large.

Braz $$ *Rua Maria Angelica, 129, tel: 2525-0687.* Open Sun–Thur 6.30pm–12.30am, Fri–Sat 6.30am–1.30am. With the atmosphere of a typical 1920s Italian cantina, Braz quickly became one of Rio's leading pizza houses on opening in 2007. Considered by many to serve the city's best pizza. Very popular so expect to have to wait in line.

Jockey Club $$$ *Centro Gastronomico Victoria, Rua Mario Ribeiro, 410, tel: 2540-9017.* Open daily 8pm–1am. Despite being located within the Jockey Club, this elegant but relaxed gastronomic centre is open to one and all. It offers a good mix of traditional dishes, pizzas and Japanese cuisine from which diners can pick and choose. The large veranda offers views across the racecourse to Corcovado. Go on a race day to enjoy the horses racing past nearby.

Olympe (Claude Troisgros) $$$$$ *Rua Custódio Serrão, 62, tel: 2539-4542.* Open 7pm–midnight, lunch Fri, closed Sun. From one of France's most traditional gastronomic families, Claude Troisgros has been one of Brazil's culinary gods since arriving in Rio in the early 1980s. He expertly combines French and Brazilian influences and Olympe is his flagship. Reservations a must.

Palaphita Kitch $$ *Av. Epitácio Pessoa (Kiosk 20 – Parque do Cantagalo), tel: 2227-0837.* Open daily 6pm–3am. When the shores around the Lagoa were redeveloped in 2004, Rio had a new option for eating and drinking: the kiosks that spread around the lake to varying degrees of sophistication. This is one of the best and most popular, situated in front of Parque do Cantagalo. A stunning location to enjoy a limited menu of Amazonian and contemporary dishes.

INDEX

Berlitz pocket guide

Rio de Janeiro

Eighth Edition 2008

Written by Ken Bernstein
Updated by Chris Pickard
Series Editor: Tony Halliday

Printed in Singapore by Insight Print
Services (Pte) Ltd, 38 Joo Koon Road,
Singapore 628990. Tel: (65) 6865-1600.
Fax: (65) 6861-6438

Berlitz Trademark Reg. U.S. Patent Office
and other countries. Marca Registrada

Photography credits
AKG London 15; Maria de Fatima Campos and
Richard Davis 7, 9, 10, 13, 17, 18, 23, 24, 26, 28,
30, 31, 33, 34, 35, 36, 37, 39, 40, 41, 42, 45, 46,
47, 48, 51, 55, 56, 57, 61, 62, 65, 66, 72, 74, 79,
80, 82, 84, 85, 86, 88, 90, 93, 94, 96; Eric Carl
Font/APA 59, 71, 89, 97; Vange Millet, courtesy
of Museu Paulista USP 20; Vange Millet, courtesy
of Aceno Galeria de Arte 21; Neil Schlecht 6,
52, 68

Cover picture: Günter Gräfenhain/
4Corners Images

Every effort has been made to provide
accurate information in this publication,
but changes are inevitable. The publisher
cannot be responsible for any resulting
loss, inconvenience or injury.

Contact us

At Berlitz we strive to keep our guides as
accurate and up to date as possible, but if you
find anything that has changed, or if you have
any suggestions on ways to improve this guide,
then we would be delighted to hear from you.

Berlitz Publishing, PO Box 7910,
London SE1 1WE, England.
fax: (44) 20 7403 0290
email: berlitz@apaguide.co.uk
www.berlitzpublishing.com